# ▸ Testimonials

"Nicky Kalliongis worked for me at Arista Records for seventeen years. He was unfailingly ready and eager to pitch in at all times with a smile and infectious enthusiasm. Mainly doing studio A&R work, often in editing album cuts to singles length and structure, Nicky was always a pleasure and a dedicated, hard worker."
**—Clive Davis, Chairman & CEO, BMG, U.S.**

"Nicky Kalliongis, better known as "Nick the Cat," is one of the premier music executives in the country. With over 20 years in the business, Nicky has participated in the success of the world's biggest acts including Whitney Houston, Toni Braxton, Aretha Franklin, Carlos Santana, and Prince. His tremendous work ethic, attention to detail, and superb musical instincts truly exemplifies him as one of the top A&R men in the business today."
**—Monte Lipman, President, Universal Records**

"I've known and worked with Nicky on numerous projects over the last 10 years from superstar artist releases to independent developing artists. Nicky has contributed to many hit records across all levels of the business and his experience stretches from the multi-national recording company to the indie. It is exciting to see him stay current and even ahead of the game by bringing his expertise of music into the digital space."
**—George Levendis, Senior Vice President Global Marketing, SONY BMG Music Entertainment**

"During the heyday of the New York music biz in the late '80s and early '90s, one of the best seats in the house was huddled together in the Arista A&R Department around Clive Davis. It was there that Nicky and our A&R team oversaw in great detail some of the finest contemporary pop records made, deciding who to sign, what song to give to which artist and with which music producer. It was a place and a time that was just magical. We all brought our special expertise from different areas and one of Nicky K's was the studio. Nicky was splicing and dicing Whitney Houston in the AM or the Grateful Dead in the afternoon so that all of America would have something special on their radio come Monday morning. Nicky's pop music instincts made our music come to life in a brilliant collage kind of way and it all made perfect pop sense."
**—Richard Sweret, former Senior VP A&R BMG International Former VP Arista A&R**

## ► About The Author

Nicky Kalliongis is an accomplished musician and music technician in addition to being a seasoned music industry professional with expertise in the area of Artist and Repertoire. Reporting directly to Clive Davis, the Founder, former chairman and CEO of Arista Records, Mr. Kalliongis was responsible for evaluating new music on behalf of Davis as well as iden-tifying, developing, and editing numerous hit songs that have achieved Gold, Platinum and Multi-Platinum status. To date he has been involved in over 653 Platinum Albums, an astounding achievement of 653 million plus in record sales.

Nicky Kalliongis originated the idea of an in-house digital editing station, implementing the technology that resulted in significant time and cost savings while eliminating creative lag time. He has also written music for hit T.V. shows like *Lifestyles of the Rich and Famous* and *Loving* and has appeared on MTV offering his expertise on the *100 Greatest Voices Of All Time*. In addition he has made appearances on MTV's *The Real World*.

He continues to be active in the music industry working alongside Clive Davis, L.A. Reid, Monte Lipman and others.

# MYSPACE MUSIC PROFIT MONSTER!

Proven Online Music Marketing Strategies!

www.MySpaceMusicProfitMonster.com

Nicky Kalliongis

MTV Press

First MTV Press Edition published April 2008
ISBN: 978-1-57687-446-2
Library of Congress Control Number: 2007941983
MTV Press and all related titles, logos, and characters are trademarks of MTV
Networks, a division of Viacom International Inc.

# ►Table Of Contents

# ► Introduction

In a world where people had been accustomed to asking, "What's your phone number?" they are now asking, "What's your MySpace?"

If you have always dreamed of a career in music, you're about to discover exactly how you can leverage over 100 million MySpace users to market your music. The Internet has levelled the playing field, offering more opportunities than ever before to expose your music to the world.

Of course, it all starts with the artist and the music. If the artist and the song are great, and the public is made aware through marketing and promotional efforts, then you have the beginnings of a superstar and a mega hit.

What makes an artist great? I have always looked for artists that have a strong identity and offer a singular point of view. A powerful point of view gives an artist a strong chance of influencing pop culture. Think Dylan, Aretha, Springsteen, U2, or Whitney. I have to feel that an artist has impact, and that the songs and performances are great. Whether that talent is raw or seasoned, it is these qualities that separate the superstars from everybody else.

This book is not about the music or the artist, however. This book is for the artist or independent record label confident they have what it takes and eager to take a proactive approach in their career. It's for the artist that wants to say to the world, "Here I am!"

In this book you'll learn the exact steps to effective music marketing on MySpace, and how to synergize with other social networking sites like YouTube and Facebook so millions of people discover you and your music. You can't rely on MySpace alone. You must take an integrated approach, even if the goal is simply to drive traffic to your MySpace page. The strategies you'll learn here are "actionable," meaning you can start applying them right away.

As someone with intimate knowledge of the music business, I can tell you first hand how competitive it can be. I also know how much people want to succeed. Successfully marketing yourself online requires deliberation and purpose. Doing so will help you build a solid fan base and get you on the radar of record labels, music producers, booking agents and other music executives. And if your goal is maintaining independence, controlling your music and the money, this book will help you do that as well. Never before has the independent artist had as much control of their own destiny. The Internet is not just a promotional tool, but a distribution system as well. Using the strategies outlined in this book, you will effectively have your own built-in marketing and promotion department. In essence, your own record label.

Navigating your way through the Internet can be a huge task. Since there are many opportunities to showcase your music, advertise upcoming gigs, and generate interest online, where do you begin and which avenues are the best for you?

In this new era of online communication, social networking has become the front runner in music promotion. While radio stations and music labels are still the dominant forces behind many successful artists, people are finding other ways to discover great music. They are also listening to their music in different ways. Music can be downloaded from the Internet, people can subscribe to podcasts or Internet radio webcasts, and they can watch video clips on their computers and mobile devices.

Many musicians, even famous ones, are using the Internet as a way to attract more fans. Music that is played on the radio has been chosen by radio DJ's and music supervisors. Instead of relying solely on radio and music stores when looking for music, people can discover and instantly download the types of music they want to hear.

In this book, you will find valuable information about the benefits of using MySpace, the free social networking site that attracts millions of new visitors each day, and you'll learn all about viral marketing. You will learn how to create a MySpace profile page that attracts many visitors, how to market your music on MySpace, and how to use other social networking sites in conjunction with MySpace in order to build an even larger fan base.

What is viral marketing? Viral marketing is the online equivalent to the most potent kind of marketing, word of mouth. With viral marketing, the online message is so infectious that it creates a buzz that spreads like a virus recommending your music. It has never been easier to generate such incredible promotion and marketing as it is now.

Even though MySpace is the undisputed champion of social networking sites, it is not the only one on the Internet. In order to be successful these days, you will have to create profile pages on other networking sites like Facebook and upload video clips on YouTube.

These sites are excellent avenues for you to upload music and facts about your music, your band, and events you may be participating in. While these web sites can help you gain exposure, you may find it difficult to get the attention of visitors because of the thousands of other profile pages available for visitors to view.

This book will show you how to increase your exposure on these sites, how to drive traffic to them, and how to maintain interest for viewers and fans. The attention span online is far shorter than Television and Radio. You'll have a split second to capture the visitor's attention, and then you'll have to make sure you keep them interested and coming back. It's not enough these days to create pages on these sites and hope people will find you. Being proactive will generate more interest.

I have also provided codes at the back of this book that are very helpful with MySpace and other social networking sites.

Learning how to build a web site that highlights your music, and learning how to advertise on the Internet through online articles, blogs, podcasts, RSS feeds and forums are also important marketing strategies that will help you succeed. I can't stress how important it is to maintain a high profile online. You can achieve this by writing articles, press releases, uploading content to your web site, uploading songs to be played on podcasts, create your own webcast, and uploading video to the Internet via YouTube, MySpace, Facebook, and your own web site. Diligence, patience, and a faith in your music are what you will need in order to make a lasting impression both online and off.

In later sections of this book, you will learn how to build a web site that provides updates about events, band members, and other information fans are curious to know. You can also sell your music that will not only help you become more recognized for your talents, but can also help you pay the bills, increase gigs, and help you find a record label. If your goal is to get a record deal as opposed to being independent, record labels definitely operate today from a "show me what you got" perspective.

It's important to build a web site that reflects who you are as a musician and as a person. Your web site should be easy to navigate and contain relevant information, pictures, and songs that fans and others want to see and listen to. Updating your web site often is crucial.

Once you have your web site up and running, or have created profile pages on one or more social networking sites, you will have to begin a marketing campaign. This is where many people get scared – they feel they don't have the time or the talent to produce quality articles, press releases, and other content. I have included many tips, guidelines, and strategies in this book to help you create marketing materials like a pro.

One of the best ways to drive traffic to your web site and to profile pages on social networking sites is by writing online articles that promote your music, the industry, or anything else that fans find interesting. Not only will you increase traffic to these areas, you will also build a larger fan base by reaching select markets online. Articles are distributed all over the Internet and are used in various forums and web sites. Writing a few articles could save you hours of online marketing.

One of the best article marketing sites is Squidoo. As you learn more about online marketing in this book, you will read about Squidoo, a web site that is devoted to sharing information. You will learn how to write articles that will increase your web ranking, which means your web site will be viewed by more people.

Whether you know very little about web marketing, or more than most, this book can help you increase your online marketing presence.

Initially this book was not going to include information at the beginner level, in particular with the process of signing up and plugging in the right information and keywords, until we realized that most people were doing it all wrong! So I encourage you to read all the chapters. It is that important to have a strong foundation. Armed with this solid background you will be able to proceed to the more advanced strategies in this book.

You have the talent and drive to succeed. Learning how to use the Internet to your advantage and help your career along is the goal of this book as it contains everything you need to know about starting a music career with the help of the Internet.

As someone with over 20 years in the music business, I have been blessed to have worked with some of the most famous artists in the world including Whitney Houston, Usher, OutKast, The Rolling Stones, Avril Lavigne, and Santana. I've been very fortunate to work closely alongside Clive Davis, L.A. Reid, Monte Lipman and countless others, who I am very grateful and indebted to. I have seen the way the music business has changed over the years and I understand the stress and pressure you are under when you want to succeed in doing something you are passionate about.

I wrote this book to help and inform people just like you so you can take advantage of everything this new technology has to offer.

Now let's get started!

P.S. Congratulations on reading this book! It means you're a doer and that alone will set you miles ahead in the game since most people never take action!

## Chapter 1

# ► The Social Networking Boom

During its infancy, the Internet was used primarily for the exchange of text files. There were no colorful or flashy web pages. You would simply open up Notepad, scribble some words, and email the attachment to a friend. Things have changed in ways few of us could have anticipated.

The engine driving the Internet is millions of consumers looking for goods, services, and entertainment. With its rapid growth ever-more homes and businesses are hooked up to the web with access to communication portals that simply weren't available five or ten years ago. For those in the music industry and those struggling to get in this means conventional approaches to music promotion are in flux.

With more people using the Internet to communicate, download new music, or watch user-generated videos, you have an exciting advantage—the ability to create a larger fan base in a much shorter amount of time.

## WHAT IS SOCIAL NETWORKING?

Social networking sites have been around for several years, but it wasn't until the success of MySpace that people began to utilize them for more than casual conversation. Other sites like Facebook and YouTube have followed the success of MySpace by allowing people to upload video, podcasts, and more. In the Web 2.0 era, you can upload music, photos, and stay in constant contact with fans and those in the music industry.

There are many different components to social networking sites, but most of them share the following:

- The ability to create a network of online friends

- The ability to communicate with people all over the world

- The ability to customize profiles and create a steady web presence

Establishing a web presence is the most important way to generate interest in your music. Use the Internet properly, and you can reach many people at one time, and share your music. You will also be able to catch the attention of music producers and labels.

Sites like MySpace, YouTube, and Facebook rely on users to provide the content that keeps visitors coming back. It's simple and it works. MySpace is growing at a rate of over 230,000 new members every day and approximately 32 billion page views a month. Such rapid growth is what makes these web sites the perfect platform for your musical ambition.

Through the use of these sites, you will be able to connect with more people without having to rely on selective broadcasters. Social networking incorporates the modern day belief that Internet users should be able to share information freely and choose what they want.

If you haven't already jumped on the networking bandwagon, there is no better time than now. Throughout this book, you will learn many ways to promote your music and reach millions of people. You will also learn how to use social networking sites properly in order to attract producers and record labels.

## DECLINE OF THE MAINSTREAM BROADCASTER

The boom of social networking and user-generated content has given musicians the ability to create their own fan base without having to rely solely on radio stations and television. With advances like podcasting and streaming video, you can have your music played all over the world without having to worry about signing a recording contract or even releasing a CD.

The music industry is desperately, if not slowly, trying to reinvent itself in order to embrace the digital revolution. With illegal downloads a serious threat to record labels, the need for a legal alternative is urgent.

The growth of MySpace and YouTube demonstrates that more and more people are visiting these sites in order to hear unknown artists to see what they have to offer. In the past people were told what to watch and what to listen to. Internet users can log on to their favorite sites and download music or videos. In this era, it's anything at anytime.

An independent artist looking to take advantage of this movement has myriad ways to market his/her music online. Uploading your songs and videos to sites like MySpace and YouTube gives visitors a chance to listen to your music if they want to. The boundaries of mainstream music have become much broader because of the choices people have online. Because of this, it's possible to get recognition for your music by developing a dedicated fan base through social networking web sites.

As a result, the Internet has shifted the balance of power from radio and television. Radio broadcasters and others have had to change their tactics in order to compete with the growing online music industry. Online visitors are being exposed to an increasingly diverse range of work and it's all because musicians have seen how this form of music promotion can influence their careers.

People can now choose what they want to hear. There are thousands of pages on the Internet devoted to music. They can also choose what they want to watch—and if the broadcaster isn't willing to air it, people can find web sites that will.

As you can see, there are radical changes taking place that you should be participating in when trying to promote your music. Creating profile pages on MySpace, YouTube, and Facebook and using them together will enable you to reach a diverse market. Each networking site caters to somewhat different markets. Make your music available to each market and your fan base will grow.

## WAYS TO MARKET YOUR MUSIC ONLINE

In addition to social networking sites like MySpace, YouTube, and Facebook, musicians are finding other ways to get their music heard as well. These include:

- Dedicated web site

- Podcasting

- Streaming video

- Music sites

- Article marketing

- Blogging

Using these marketing tools along with social networking sites will enable you to reach more listeners. Remember that it is much easier to promote a band or solo artist that already has a following. If you promote your music and create a strong fan base, you will get the attention of the music industry.

In later chapters, I will show you how to use the above marketing tools to increase traffic to your site and to pages you create on networking sites. These tools are very useful if you want to sell your music online.

## POWER TO THE PEOPLE

Now that people have more control over what they listen to, it is up to you to give them quality music that resonates with them. It is also important to entertain your fans by updating your web site, uploading new songs, creating a blog, and engaging them in other ways so they develop a loyalty to you. There is an ongoing audience that is willing to listen and judge your work. If you're the next big thing, and you can market your music so it's heard, chances are you'll get noticed and acknowledged for it.

Chapter 2

# ▸ Why Artists Are Turning To MySpace and Other Marketing Sites

Now that we know why social networking sites are critical to expanding the audience for your music, it's time to start establishing your presence on them. The three sites you need to get your campaign rolling are:

- MySpace

- YouTube

- Facebook

Why:

- Online marketing is cost effective, requiring only time and effort in most cases

- Communicate with a diverse array of people

- Reach new audiences quickly

- Sell your music

- Easier access to labels and industry executives

Marketing via social networking sites is no longer an alternative to or enhancement of traditional marketing. It's becoming the norm. Even for established and iconic artists and bands it's become standard.

## MYSPACE

MySpace was the first large, free music arena to be created on the Internet. Millions of people visit and create profile pages each year. With so many people taking advantage of MySpace to jumpstart their music career or further it, you have to be "marketing savvy" in order to be noticed. You can't expect potential fans to stumble upon you. You have to draw them in.

Throughout this book, you will find tips along with online resources that will give you an edge over those who know little about online marketing. Use them and you will quickly see the results.

# REASONS TO USE MYSPACE

If you've done your research—and that's never a bad thing in this business—you have probably noticed that there are many alternatives to MySpace. These include Facebook, YouTube, Blogger, Friendster and so on. In later chapters, I will offer tips on using Facebook, YouTube, and the online marketing site Squidoo to really boost your exposure online.

When it comes to choosing which sites to focus on, I urge you to use all three. Promoting your music solely on MySpace is not enough these days. Because so many musicians have taken advantage of MySpace, getting recognized for your work is ever more difficult. Making use of all three networking sites will give you added exposure and allow those who don't visit MySpace a chance to hear your music.

MySpace attracts roughly 230,000 new members every single day. It's an astonishing number and one you should not ignore.

Of course, it should be noted that many of MySpace's features require a user to be logged in. I can't say for sure that all of those 230,000 users are going to remain active, but it is fair to assume many will.

Another remarkable statistic is that MySpace is the sixth most visited English-language web site in the world. That makes it the most active of the social networking sites.

I should warn you not to forget about other marketing sites, as they will also increase your fan base and add value by putting you in touch with specific groups who will become loyal listeners. Try to get a vibe from the site to see who it is catering to and which direction it is going.

Almost every band has a MySpace profile or uses other networking including well known bands and artists like U2, Coldplay, Alicia Keys, 50 Cent, Kanye West, Rascal Flatts, Fall Out Boy, Jay-Z, etc. You can throw in just about every other band of significance (or not). One of the great incentives for joining is the connection to superstars. Can you imagine the massive boost of being displayed next to the world's biggest bands on the MySpace homepage? It can happen. It's happened to others.

MySpace treats its members to an equal playing field and if you generate a positive viral buzz, you'll find that you can get on the MySpace homepage by taking advantage of blogging features, a widely supported messaging system with event tracking. MySpace even has its own instant messenger.

When News Corp bought MySpace for $580 million, many doubted whether the investment would prove to be a sound business decision. But the money merely adds to the suggestion that this is a business where serious profit can be made for everyone.

You don't have to pay a penny to set up a MySpace account, which will allow you to invest in a web site, paid online marketing, and other costs for your band.

# THE PRICE OF EXPOSURE

How much would it cost to advertise your product to a million people internationally? Hundreds, thousands, tens of thousands of dollars? And how many people are you likely to win over in exchange for that expense? Unless you have a secret technique that the rest of us haven't heard about, the answer is "a tiny percentage."

Record labels spend excessive amounts of money promoting bands. Whether it's through station posters or television commercials, they do everything in their power to make an impression and get people listening.

Traditional methods of generating exposure include television, radio, magazines and word of mouth. Until now, word of mouth was only valid if someone bought your album or went to your concert. But with networking sites like MySpace, word of mouth can spread quickly by uploading one song for people to hear.

How much does it cost to get a friend to say "Wow! Check out this band!" And how much of an effect is that likely to have on a consumer when purchasing an album?

Marketing gurus have always preached that word of mouth is the biggest marketing tool you can use. If you have people openly praising your product, it resonates much louder than other forms of advertising.

I could review the cost of gaining mainstream exposure via orthodox means. But can you afford to pay such inflated prices? You'd have much greater success attracting fans online.

Some of the most effective marketing in the world today is done online. Create an effective marketing campaign using networking sites, publishing articles and press releases online, and more in order to promote your music. An effective campaign will persuade people to listen to your music so they can tell their friends. This is how word of mouth spreads.

Don't take this as a backlash against traditional means. If you can combine your marketing efforts with others, your chances of success will be much greater. Social networking sites are a solid foundation you can use to build your fan base and get people talking about your music without having to spend a lot of money.

# MYSPACE SUCCESS STORIES

At this point, you may be wondering if there are any famous bands or artists that have been discovered on sites like MySpace. Below you will find a few success stories from those who used MySpace as a tool to promote their music and have earned recognition in the industry.

Clearly sites like MySpace are likely to expand far beyond the success they are currently enjoying in order to give artists even more tools they can use to launch their careers.

- The Arctic Monkeys are a product of the MySpace phenomenon. When they exploded onto the British music scene in 2005, it was largely due to the viral buzz that they generated on MySpace. The band was signed to a lofty record deal after using MySpace to promote their music. They've enjoyed widespread critical acclaim and tremendous sales—all thanks to an explosion in popularity on an Internet web site. Had it not been for MySpace, The Arctic Monkeys might still be struggling with small-time gigs. They could still be working full-time in the dead end jobs that so many of us are desperate to escape. Use MySpace as a way to generate buzz, earn more fans, and get some attention from record labels.

- Lily Allen's musical rise was initiated through her MySpace web site. She already had a record deal, but it wasn't until the MySpace community took notice that she started to enjoy real success. She used MySpace to increase her fan base.

If U2, Coldplay, Alicia Keys, and Jay-Z feel it's necessary to be active on MySpace, so should you.

## YOUTUBE

YouTube debuted in 2005 and is a social networking site that you can use to promote your music in the form of video. By promoting your music this way, fans, record labels, and others will be able to see you perform in addition to hearing the music. This is as close as people can get to hearing you live.

In addition to uploading video, you can upload a daily video blog, chat with fans and friends, and view other videos as a way to check out what's popular. Those who are registered have the opportunity to vote on videos they like and videos they don't, which you can use to gauge where you need to make improvements.

The most important thing to remember is to upload quality video clips. On the site, there are tips about setting up a shoot, which equipment to use, and how to perfect lighting and sound quality. But at the end of the day it's not the technical quality of your video, it's getting your song or message across in a way that connects with fans.

First impressions are important, so make sure you upload a video that represents you and your music, or what the vibe of the band is. You have to work 10 times as hard for a second chance.

## WHO'S USING YOUTUBE?

According to Nielsen Ratings, YouTube receives over 20 million viewers each month. Among these viewers are those who want to find more music just like yours. Take advantage of this site and everything it has to offer in order to get as much exposure as possible.

It seems that everyone from upcoming musicians to politicians trying to get the word out about their latest campaign is using YouTube. It has been estimated that 65,000 new clips are uploaded onto the web site each day. This means that while you have a large audience to play for, you also have a lot of competition.

The good news is that the marketing strategies taught in this book can be applied to any online marketing site. Uploading your video clip is not enough to generate a buzz. Constantly updating your video clips, adding new ones, and creating a blog will get people talking.

## SUCCESS STORIES ON YOUTUBE

As with MySpace, there have been many success stories built on You-Tube.

- OK Go created a sensation with their clever video for "Here It Goes Again," turning the song into a number one hit at radio and walking off with a VMA. The video has had more than 25 million plays on YouTube alone.

- Sick Puppies had one of their songs used in the background of a Free Hugs Campaign video. That video has had more than 20 million plays and the song and the band have enjoyed significant success as a result.

Once you have achieved some recognition on YouTube, your popularity will continue to grow. YouTube has created an awards show that recognizes talent and online popularity. There are also public events that viewers host to celebrate the diverse culture that continues to thrive online.

## FACEBOOK

At the time of writing, Facebook is enjoying a huge explosion in popularity. If you are looking to join online networking groups, upload video and photos, and promote upcoming events, then Facebook is the place to do it. If you are trying to attract those who are in college or who have recently graduated, Facebook is an excellent forum because it has over 19 million registered users.

## THE BENEFITS OF FACEBOOK

Facebook is different from MySpace and YouTube because you have more power in limiting who is allowed to see your home page and everything you upload on it. While you can allow anyone to view your profile page, your home page can be restricted to friends, those who belong to the same online groups, or those who ask to be included in your friends list.

With Facebook, you can:

- Upload video and photos

- Post upcoming gigs and other events

- Create a blog

- Share stories and other information with those in the groups you join

- Network with other musicians and people working in the music industry

- Use flyers to promote upcoming gigs and other news

- Add apps to your profile that feature other social networking sites where your work is featured

- Take advantage of Facebook mobile

This networking site is a little more sophisticated than other sites because of the privacy settings and group atmosphere.

## SOCIAL NETWORKING

Use Facebook to meet others in the music industry by joining specific groups. Facebook has hundreds of open forums you can join in order to make connections, find out the latest in industry news, or learn more about the industry itself.

Since there are many smaller record labels out there trying to attract new talent, learning as much as you can about them will help your chances of earning a contract. Smaller labels are constantly looking for new talent to put their company on the map, so to speak. Meeting other musicians who have these connections is a great way to get noticed by these labels and others.

Through networking, you can meet local musicians, local fans, and be able to announce where and when you will be playing.

As Facebook continues to grow, new features are being added. You can now import your external blog to the site to connect your web site. Those who are included on your friends list will be able to visit your web site and learn even more about your music.

As with MySpace and YouTube, signing up for Facebook is free. For serious social networking with other musicians and industry leaders, create an account, post your videos and photos, and join some groups. You will meet people who share the common bond of music and you will increase your exposure online.

## SQUIDOO

Squidoo is slightly different from MySpace, YouTube, and Facebook, but it can be used to highlight profile pages, video, and blogs found on these sites as well as your own web site. This is a powerful marketing tool that's highly recommended because of its ability to:

- Improve your web ranking on search engines

- Highlight video and blogs online so others can find them

- Update easily

- Sell music and merchandise

- Post commentary, photos, and video

- Squidoo is free and easy to use.

## HOW DOES SQUIDOO WORK?

Squidoo is a web site filled with mini sites one or two pages in length. They're called 'lenses' because of their ability to highlight specific information. When you create a lens, you are creating a smaller web site about your music, which will attract a high number of people instantly.

Search engines will be able to use your lens to find your web site, which will result in higher search engine rankings. The higher the ranking, the greater the exposure.

## BENEFITS

Because of your ability to post almost anything you want in your lens, you can connect your MySpace profile, YouTube videos, and your Facebook blog so people will be able to visit all three sites if they choose. This will make finding your music much easier than using search functions found on these sites.

Squidoo gives you the opportunity to showcase many different sides of your music.

## ONE MORE WORD ABOUT SOCIAL NETWORK-ING SITES

As you can see, there are many social networking sites for you to choose from depending on the types of audiences you are searching for. Take advantage of as many as possible so your music will be reached by as many as possible. Use Squidoo as a way to promote your involvement in other sites as it will make finding your music online much easier.

Chapter 3
# ▶ Record Labels VS. Going It Alone

At some point in your career, you may have to make the decision to sign with a label or continue promoting your music on your own. This is not an easy decision, but it is one that every musician wants to make at some point in his or her career.

When deciding which direction to take, you should ask yourself the following:

- Do I want to use my marketing campaign toward catching the attention of the major record labels?

- Do I want to focus my efforts solely on catching and retaining a keen fan base?

In order to have a lasting career, the answer is probably both.

It would be foolish to look at only satisfying what you think A&R is looking for, and completely abandoning the fans that make an artist desirable. At the same time, if you only work toward grabbing the attention of fans, you're likely to get lost in the sea of semi-popular unsigned artists. It is vital to have your own identity.

In this chapter, we'll be looking at the benefits of both approaches and helping you to make a decision relevant to your needs. It will most definitely affect the way in which you operate both as a businessperson and as a musician.

## TO SIGN OR NOT TO SIGN

It may seem like an easy decision to make at first. After all, the major record labels have the power and money to put you on the map and help you have a successful career. A label will handle distribution and marketing while you focus on your music. This can take a lot of pressure off musicians.

But for every band that makes it, hundreds will never see a record contract. And of the bands that have signed, very few will actually have an impact. Even if they attract the interest of a major label and sign a contract, their music might never even get released.

# THE BENEFITS OF "GOING IT ALONE"

Many independent musicians have quietly been making money selling their own work at gigs or through their web sites.

It's never been easier to distribute your own music and combine it with a solid marketing campaign.

Depending on how you market your music, you may be able to enjoy just as much success as you would if you signed a record contract.

While some of the larger, more influential bands on today's music scene make huge profits through their music sales, they also make their money through touring and merchandise sales.

If you choose to pursue a music career without a label backing you, you will keep more of the pie for yourself. In fact, you own that pie! In addition, the creative decisions are yours alone.

By going it alone, you can choose how you want to do business and control the image you want to establish, what songs to include on your album, and what artwork to use.

On the other side of the coin you can't completely write off the record labels. Not just yet. There are several advantages to signing a recording contract.

# THE BENEFITS OF SIGNING

Major labels are extremely adept at promoting music and providing the crossover opportunities that you'll need in order to become famous. If you have genuine aspirations to expand your music and reach out to an international fan base, it's likely that you're going to need a record contract at some point.

Why? For the same reason that people hire agents and public relations personnel. They take care of the stresses and strains that allow you the opportunity to focus on what you're paid for—the music.

This can come at a price, though. Record labels are very selective about the artists they sign. You might have to make the effort to conform to their preferences and to what they feel will make you the most successful. Sometimes it is an issue and sometimes it is not. For example, they may want to place your song in a television ad for cars that's going to get play on every major network and cable channel. You may be staunchly opposed to having your music used in any kind of advertising. Believe me, you will lose this battle.

When you sign a recording contract, you are required to work within certain boundaries. You'll be required to finish any recording on a schedule. You'll be required to tour at an appropriate time and make promotional appearances on a schedule set by the company, all based on when they release your music.

Record labels also don't want to sign you on the basis of a demo or a particular sound, only to have a completely different sound when you've finished the first album.

Most artists have an identifiable sound so it will probably not be an issue. But if you decide to change your sound at some point, and there is a disagreement with the label and your contract states they have final say, you might find it problematic.

## HAVING IT ALL

Even in this era where it seems the power of labels is slipping, there are still a lot of very positive things that a major label can do for you and your music.

How do you decide which route is better for you, your music, and your career?

It's important to decide what you want and what you are capable of accomplishing. It's also important to try different avenues to see which is the best for you. Chances are you're reading this because you don't have a contract lined up. Instead of focusing all of your energies on finding a label, this book will teach you to succeed on your own. You may never become rich and famous, but you can make a good living doing what you love. For many people this is enough. But if you feel that you need the security of a record label taking over the marketing and distribution duties, it's important to market your music in such a way that it is inviting to prospective labels.

## MAINSTREAM CROSSOVER OPPORTUNITIES

Perhaps the greatest benefit of having a major record deal comes in the form of mainstream exposure. Below are the key areas in which a label will ease your promotional burden.

- Television
- Radio
- Magazines and Newspapers
- Retail

Labels are staffed with experienced professionals in the areas of marketing, publicity and radio promotion who work together to maximize the visibility of you and your music.

The marketing team works well in advance of an album's release to generate buzz. The work a single early, getting it onto key web sites, on hip mixtapes, and maybe even into an iPod commercial.

The radio promotions team hits the appropriate format to gain airplay for the song in different markets across the country. Some songs that appear to be overnight successes may have begun playing in a single market six months before quietly building a substantial audience and demonstrating to other radio programmers in other cities that they should be playing the song as well.

I probably don't have to tell you too much about what publicists do but, suffice it to say, they know every nook and cranny that can help establish an artist. That covers influential industry publications you may not have heard of to a tour of tastemaker independent record shops.

Each of these teams has knowledge, contacts and relationships that take years to acquire. Unless you are independently wealthy or making a ton of money from your music already, hiring independent companies to perform these functions on your behalf is not likely.

## TELEVISED APPEARANCES

Without a contract, it's extremely difficult to get prime bookings for television shows, radio spots, and other mass marketing media. You've probably seen chat shows with guest musical performances. Most of these are arranged through the record label, usually to promote an upcoming album or a tour.

Such opportunities are important for up and coming performers. It's a chance to be seen by millions and the televised aspect helps to convey an image of mass appeal.

With radio, it can sometimes be difficult to distinguish between bands. People will often hum along to a tune without knowing who performed it. While this is still important, it certainly helps to have a televised performance where the audience gets to see the faces behind the sound.

## RADIO INTERVIEWS

Radio shows can be a good source of publicity too. Record labels can organize interviews with radio hosts, maybe to introduce a new song or for a brief topical discussion of a new record. All of this exposure helps you get your name out there.

I should note that it's also possible to get radio bookings as an independent artist. Also the new boom of pod-casting has paved the way for thousands of low budget shows. You can become a part of it and share some of the spotlight. Pod-casting relies on computers and iPods as a way to transmit sound in the form of mp3 recordings. This is good news for aspiring musicians. Of course, it isn't as mainstream as traditional radio broadcasts, but it's a great place to start.

## MAGAZINES, ONLINE PUBLICATIONS AND PRESS RELEASES

Have you ever wondered how recently signed bands end up in major music magazines? Most of the time, it's because of the direct contact between a record label and the publishers of the magazine.

Millions of music fans read magazines and online articles on their favorite stars. It's a great source for finding new talent, and a brilliant place to showcase your hard work.

Record companies will do their best to make sure that your work gets reviewed. They'll even encourage the journalist to offer a higher score if they're particularly cosy with the publication!

Whether you are trying to market yourself without the assistance of a record label or you are trying to get the attention of a label, writing a powerful press release about your upcoming album or gig and posting it online through online newswires like PRLeap, PR9, PrWeb, ClickPress, online music promotion web sites, or in your local newspaper can help attract attention both online and off.

When writing a press release, you should:

- Keep it short (one page is plenty)

- Write about a specific topic and tie it to a specific event (holiday, season, local event, music industry news, etc.) as a way to generate more interest from news wires and other sites

- Include the search term you want to be associated with by including it in the title of your release ('Online Music Promotion' is more specific than using 'music'). Include this in the body of your release as well

Submit a few press releases a year as a way to increase traffic to your web site and increase your search engine ranking. Use a writer if you can't write them yourself.

## POWER OF THE PRESS

We've all opened up a magazine or logged on to a web site only to find a terrible band receiving accolades. The critics often have their darling artists who they convey positive images for, and you'd be a fool to under-estimate the role that the record label plays in that process.

Many artists are turned in to superstars through mainstream publicity. Getting crossover opportunities says that you're powerful. It shows that you're influential and that people have a reason to talk about you. Even if you're not as established as you'd like to be, a round of mainstream exposure can do wonders for your career.

On your own, it will be more difficult to strike up deals with the agencies that matter – at least where mainstream marketing is concerned.

But many bands rack up sales without resorting to the world of mainstream exposure. Underground scenes are still proving fruitful for many, but you have to strike up equally good contacts to be a hit that way too. You also have to work tirelessly to stay one step ahead of the game. If you are not constantly marketing your music, fans will become fickle and look elsewhere.

# CONTRACT STIPULATIONS

Once you have caught the attention of a record label, you will have to meet with producers and A&R people to talk about the direction of your music, how they want to promote you, and many other topics before you will be offered a contract.

If you get a contract, you should consider it carefully. It could be the difference between a satisfying career and frustrating creative restriction.

How costly is a contract? It's a good question and its one which you should give a great deal of thought to.

Ask yourself these questions:

- What are my motives for making music?

- Is it simply to turn a few heads and impress at live gigs?

- Do I feel creatively inclined to reinvent myself after a successful venture?

Remember that record labels are primarily interested in maximizing sales. If you have a huge hit, what's next? When you sign a contract, you may be asked to produce music that is similar over and over.

Some artists have managed to re-invent their sound while maintaining their popularity. Others have been less successful. The "One Hit Wonder" title is an unpleasant one, but it falls on many.

Record labels are extremely picky about the choices that you make as a musician. If you release a successful album and then try to change your sound, it's possible that they'll intervene or ditch you altogether.

Record contracts are often excruciatingly restrictive affairs. Here are some of the things to look out for:

- **Minimum album releases**

    They may require that you release at least three more albums. This is a long-term tie in.

- **Studio deadlines**

    Particularly on your second record, labels will impose deadlines for work to be handed over to them as it is part of the marketing cycle.

- **Radio-friendly tracks**

  Some labels have been known to heavily encourage, and even require the inclusion of tracks that they want you to record that can be handed over for radio-play.

- **Arrangement of the record**

  If it's too long or the structure is not radio friendly, you will have to make it "commercially acceptable."

- **Promotion commitments**

  Don't like the thought of travelling the circuit and promoting your latest work? Then don't sign a contract that requires public appearances at your label's discretion.

As you can see, there are several contingencies that can be somewhat irritating if you enjoy the freedom to be creative in your own time.

Do you see making music as a business rather than a passionate hobby? Or is it both? The answer to that question will help guide you in a direction that works with your goals.

In the end, it is important to recognize that a contract isn't necessarily a ticket to superstardom. Along with the many positives, there are many issues and you should thoroughly consider the offer before signing.

## WHAT'S RIGHT FOR ME?

It's very difficult for me to offer individual advice as ambitions vary dramatically among musicians. Only you know what's right for you and your music.

But I can address some considerations that will hopefully steer you in the right direction:

- **Do I want the creative license to produce music when and how I like?**

  If you feel you need flexibility over your work, going it alone may be the best option. Not only do you avoid studio deadlines, you can take breaks when you like and scrap a project if you're not happy with it. Many established artists would love to have the freedom to let the work come to them naturally.

- **Do I want to record a follow-up album?**

  If you only plan to release a single record, and it's already written, there's absolutely no reason why a record deal can't be beneficial providing they will agree to only that one record, but you have to be careful when seeking one out. The large majority of companies will have a clause stipulating that they can request follow-ups. Look for a label that is willing to take you on as a "one time only" deal. That way, you don't have to worry about writing the follow-up and you can put all your energies into the promotion of the album. Be advised that it is rare to find a major label to agree to this.

- **What if my music is too diverse to be categorized?**

    If you have a particularly broad sound, it can be hard to find a label that fulfils your needs. Most companies specialise in certain genres. If you prefer to create within several genres simultaneously, you're likely to face greater difficulty in landing a contract. Labels love to have a sound that they can promote—rather than a collection of incredibly different tracks. Consistency is an important factor they look for in an artist.

- **Do I have the time to promote my work?**

    Be honest with yourself. Marketing music isn't easy, and it isn't a process that happens quickly. To be successful on your own, you'll have to spend many hours refining a campaign and tracking its effectiveness. Of course, the eventual return is much greater if you're selling your own product without third party involvement. But to start making these sales, it's likely that you'll need a greater investment—either of time or money.

- **Are mainstream opportunities important to me?**

    If you'll settle for nothing less than the cover of *Rolling Stone*, mainstream publicity is something you will have to work very hard to achieve. Record labels are geared towards getting you this type of exposure. They have immense lists of contacts. By signing a contract you're opening up many doors. The downside is some of these opportunities can feel forced on you. If you take particular pride in your public image, and don't want to appear mainly as a public marketing tool, be careful what you sign up for. Many labels rely on their artists doing weeks of media appearances and PR boosting trips.

## BE REALISTIC

I can't stress this enough.

Be honest with the quality of your music. If your work isn't polished enough, or it doesn't check the boxes, there is no reason why you HAVE to pursue a record deal. Many people can make a healthy living selling their own work even though major companies have turned them away.

If your image isn't cut out for the rock 'n roll lifestyle, that's fine. The wonderful thing about the new digital age is that it can be absolutely faceless. You can sell songs without ever having to appear outside the studio to promote them.

Working on your own can be a rewarding experience and a genuine thrill.

# WHAT DO MAJOR LABELS LOOK FOR?

The truth is that there are no set guidelines for what a record label will look for in an artist. That's what makes the music business so wonderfully rewarding, and so painfully frustrating. You can have what everybody tells you are a wonderful set of songs, and a major label will still turn you down.

Why?

There could be a number of reasons.

I can't guarantee that you won't get shrugged off by those in the recording industry, but I can help you maximize your chances of getting their attention. There are several things that record companies assess almost instantly when looking at an artist's profile page and or web site.

- **Number of Songs on Playlist Getting Attention**

    It's highly unlikely that a record company will pursue you based on the quality of a single track. I'd never say never—it does happen, and there have been platinum album sales on the basis of one single song. But it's still unlikely. You should share at least two or three of your tracks. Preferably, you should be serving up songs that display a versatile range of musical talent within your same sound family. While it may not be obvious to the casual listener, record labels will pick up on your potential and song ability.

- **Variety of Songs**

    If you upload four catchy easy-going tracks, you might attract a legion of fans. But it is much more exciting to hear a variety of tempo and tracks. It is best to present 3 or 4 songs that display your full range of talents. Let them hear what you're capable of across the board. And make sure they're still catchy!

- **Free Songs**

    Have you made your tracks available for download? It might not be a good idea to make songs that you intend to sell available for free. Why would a record label take you on if you are already giving the music away. However if you're going at it alone, there is a strong argument to be made that by giving away your songs and getting massive fans, you make up for it from the many fans that pay to go to your performances.

- **Image**

    Your professional image is critical. Labels aren't going to be drawn to poorly designed profiles with kid's quizzes decorating the page.

Music executives like to see people who let their music do the talking. If you look at profile pages of signed acts, you'll see they're rarely complicated and often utilitarian by design with little more than a background image.

If you want to look professional, keep it simple. Don't fill your page with distracting elements. If you think you've gone too far, you have.

It's one thing to make your music compatible with a major label's specifications; it's another thing to create an image to invite their interest.

How is it possible to make yourself a target?

How can you put yourself in the midst of a bidding war for your talents?

## APPROACHING RECORD LABELS

Don't be afraid to approach record labels on your own. You could be waiting around on MySpace all year, and with such a high level of competition, you might not receive so much as a passing glance from a label.

You can, however, make yourself known by seeking out record labels. Some labels have their own MySpace profiles. View their page and contact them. Be prepared to reach out and build bridges, for there's a very good chance that one of the contacts will serve you well in the future.

Some labels don't advertise on MySpace, so you will have to do additional research to find their contact information. Just because they don't have a MySpace page doesn't mean they are not receptive to hearing your demo. Call or send an email with your web site link or MySpace profile page link along with a bio and a electronic press kit (EPK). It is important to get permission first as more and more labels do not accept unsolicited material. The link will make it easier for them to listen to your music. You can also send a CD if you have one.

Depending on the label, even after listening to your songs on MySpace, they may still ask you to submit a demo on disc.

A demo is designed to showcase your talents and advertise your sound. If you're using MySpace, your uploaded songs can be used to create a demo. All you need to do is burn three or four songs to a CD and mail it to the label.

## VIRAL MARKETING

Another tool to consider is viral marketing on MySpace. It's a good idea to get acquainted with some signed artists—even if they're on smaller labels—and use their reputation to help build your own.

One way to do this is to strike up deals with a couple of artists that have been signed by a label and ask them to display your profile in their Top 8. Record labels will see you popping up in regular places and if they happen to check you out, they may be interested in talking with you.

If you're going to use this tactic, it's absolutely vital that you target artists who create music similar to yours. There's no point in grabbing the attention of a rap-based label if you produce heavy metal.

## ATTRACTING SMALLER LABELS

Don't be afraid to express the fact that you're unsigned.

Have you any idea how many independent labels are on the lookout for enthusiastic and welcoming artists?

If you are looking for a smaller label to work with, stick a notice in your profile. State the fact that you're looking for a record deal. When an A&R scout comes along due to some kind of buzz or from seeing you name popping up in many places, they will compare your potential with the specifications they are looking for. If you show that you're talented you will find that there are more opportunities for recording contracts that you originally thought.

It is strongly recommend, however, that you avoid looking desperate. Do not post statements like:

"Please give me a contract! I need some money!"

Striking a balance between being open to smaller labels and showing that you understand what you are worth in the industry, will show labels big and small that you are a serious musician.

## GETTING ON THE FRONT PAGE

One of the best ways to attract attention from the people that matter is to have your work featured on the homepages of sites like MySpace and YouTube. It is a sign to producers, booking agents and labels that your music is popular on the site.

Front-page promotion is likely to cost you, but the results are spectacular. Receiving such exposure will lead to enormous increases in profile traffic. Make no mistake, the labels do check out those front-page listings.

MySpace regularly offers opportunities to artists and you can take full advantage if you're in the right place at the right time.

MySpace uses a randomizing script to gift free publicity to certain artists at certain times. It's an incredible bonus for those who are lucky enough to be chosen and a wild dream for everybody else.

You can also get exposure in the music sub-section by reaching the top of the MySpace charts. As a long-term goal, this is brilliant. But you should expect to be receiving heavy traffic before such chart positions are possible.

## OTHER WAYS TO ATTRACT LABELS

In addition to MySpace, YouTube, and Facebook, there are other ways that can help you attract record labels.

- Invite local radio personalities to gigs

- Invite local record label producers to gigs

- Sell a CD online and at gigs. If you are showing sales in your hometown that are extraordinary, they will notice

- Use Podcasting and other forms of digital media

Keeping people informed about your career is what will keep people coming back. You can attract a record label by having an established fan base, music that is selling well, and by becoming a steady presence on the local circuit.

Take advantage of podcasting, streaming video, and online music distributors that have the means to reach more people than you can. Producing strong music is an accomplishment that few achieve and you should be proud if you do.

These days, selling your own music and playing local gigs is enough for many musicians to earn a living. Advancing in your music career by playing often, writing songs, and living your life can help you attract a record label even when you aren't looking for one.

Chapter 4
# ▸ Joining MySpace

Now that we've looked at different marketing options available to you, it's time to learn how to create a MySpace profile page and learn more about the options you have when using this site to promote your music.

This chapter will walk you through the registration process. It will only take you five minutes to set up a new account.

So let's get to it.

*The MySpace registration screen*

## REGISTERING A MYSPACE ACCOUNT

MySpace is designed to be accessed by millions of users. As such, it is simple and easy to use.

To create a new account, go to the MySpace web site, www.myspace.com.

From the main toolbar, select the "Music" link.

Remember! You're not interested in the standard MySpace registration. Signing up as an artist is a different process altogether, so make sure you pick the right screen.

Select the "Artist Sign-Up" link in the top right hand corner.

This will bring you to the form displayed in the screenshot on the previous page. There shouldn't be too much to confuse you here, but I'll review the options:

- **Email Address**

    This is the address where your verification email and any alerts will be sent. Don't use a fake address. You won't be able to access your account unless it's genuine.

- **Band Name**

    This is the name of your band. Users will be able to find you by searching out names. It also appears in your profile and directory listings.

- **Password**

    You will need to use a password with over six characters that includes both letters and numbers.

- **Genre**

    This is an important listing as it allows users to search via a genre. If you place your act in the wrong genre, you're going to be listed in the wrong search engine results. All the major genres are listed, and many you might not have heard of. Your selection will be displayed in your profile.

- **Country**

    Select your current location.

- **Preferred Site & Language**

    This only applies to your personal browsing experience when using MySpace. There are several versions and depending on which you use, different content will be served to the prominent pages. Choosing the UK based site, for example, will display bands from the UK in the Music section headlines.

- **Terms and Conditions**

    Be sure to select the box agreeing to the terms and conditions. Click "Sign Up" and you're almost done!

Next, you'll have to enter image verification keys. They're a necessary precaution to prevent robots spamming on MySpace.

| Sign Up! | |
|---|---|
| Your MySpace URL: | myspace.com/ myband |
| | (e.g. http://www.myspace.com/yourbandname) |
| Genre 1: | Alternative |
| Genre 2: | Indie |
| Genre 3: | Acoustic |
| Website: : | http://www.mywebsite.com |
| Current Record Label: : | unsigned |
| Label Type: : | Unsigned |
| | Continue |

*The registration phase, Step 2*

The following page will look something like the above. Of course, you can expect the fields to be empty with the exception of the MySpace URL which will already be filled with your default band name.

The MySpace URL is an important one. You shouldn't give yourself an obscure URL, so choose one the represents your band.

If you can't have MySpace.com/MyBand, go for something appropriate along the lines of.

- MyBandOfficial

- OfficialMyBand

- MyBandSpace

You'll also be given the chance to select two sub-genres. This is a great opportunity to get your music listed in more directories, so use them, even if your music only fits one category.

Be as accurate as possible with genre descriptions. If this isn't possible, go for two of the less popular choices. You might not be appealing to the right bunch of fans, but you're more likely to get noticed in a genre that isn't filled with millions of other similar acts.

"Record Label" is self-explanatory.

The final box "Label Type" has three choices.

- **Major**

    If you're signed to a major label choose "Major."

- **Indie**

    There are still plenty of reputable Indie labels around, although they don't necessarily possess the same clout as the major labels. If you're an Indie label or signed to one, choose Indie.

- **Unsigned**

  The musical equivalent of being single.

Once you're happy with your details, submit them and move on to the image upload page.

MySpace visitors tend to like images. It's sensible to let your fans get a glimpse of you. This is, after all, a social networking web site!

Use the "upload" function to add a photo to your profile and in search listings. In fact, it'll show up just about everywhere that your name appears on the site, so try and make it a good representation of you or your band.

Click "Skip Now" if you don't have any photos you want to upload.

Next, you'll now be offered the chance to invite friends to MySpace.

For now, I'll skip the friends section and the "Add Songs" screen until later in the book. There I will discuss ways to increase your friends list and how to add songs that will generate more interest on MySpace.

You'll now be taken to your MySpace profile management screen. Any new alerts will be displayed here, and you can use the options to navigate the rest of the site. You already have a new message from Tom, who is one of the original owners of the MySpace web site.

*The MySpace account management screen*

Above is what you'll see when you view the account management screen for the first time. Of course, your URL will be different and your name will be pasted in the greeting heading.

- **Edit Profile**

    This takes you to the profile editing screen. I'll go over it in detail later. For now, this is where the major customization takes place.

- **Safe Mode**

  If you somehow manage to wreck your profile with erroneous code, enter Safe Mode and fix the HTML without additional formatting.

- **Account Settings**

  This controls the bare essentials of your MySpace account. It has the privacy settings, your current email, and any additional options which let you customize your browsing experience.

- **Upload/Change Photos**

  As you'd expect, this is where you can add photos to your gallery. You can also change the default profile image and even add a photo to be ranked.

- **Add/Change Videos**

  Making use of the MySpace video player, this menu allows you to change videos and upload new files.

- **Edit Comments**

  If you are abused by rogue MySpace users feel free to delete their comments. Negative publicity isn't particularly desirable, although if you're enjoying a successful period, a stray rebel can help boost support from your fans.

- **Manage Calendar**

  This lets you keep track of what you have planned. It can also be used to alert you to certain dates in the future.

- **Manage Blog**

  I'll discuss blogging later in another chapter, but this is where you control your profile blog and its access permissions.

- **Manage Address Book**

  This lets you keep track of the people that you've contacted.

Further down the page, you'll see a box with four options marked "My Mail." This is the inbox for your account, It also handles other requests.

- **Inbox**

  When you have a "New Messages" alert, click your inbox to read them.

- **Friend Requests**

  If somebody tries to add you as a friend, you'll receive notification and this link will take you to the request management screen. You can either approve or decline friendship. I recommend that you approve everybody who wants to be added to your list.

- **Sent**

  This folder contains all your sent items. It will also state whether the mail has been read. "Sent" means that the user hasn't opened it. "Read" means that they have. "Replied" means that they've read and replied to it.

- **Post Bulletin**

  This link takes you to the bulletin creation page. I'll explain it in greater detail later on.

Once you start adding friends, you'll notice that their bulletins are displayed under the mailbox.

## VALIDATION AND CONFIRMATION

Having registered your MySpace account, you'll notice an alert on the homepage with a message stating "Verify your email address." Click the alert and select the "Verify Email" option.

This is a necessary step in order to access the full array of MySpace features.

To validate your account, simply log in to your email client and open the mail titled "MySpace Account Confirmation."

Inside you'll find a link to verify that the account belongs to you. Click this link then log in with the details already provided. Your account has been activated and you're ready to use MySpace.

## INVITING FRIENDS

It's important to immediately tap into the many marketing tools offered by MySpace. This is a social networking web site and by all means, you should be marketing yourself so your music will stand out from the rest. Having a bunch of real life friends added to your profile will not only add to the activity that you receive, but it'll boost your reputation immediately.

Casual MySpace browsers like to see that others have already discovered you. It's important that you invite your close contacts, and MySpace has a feature designed for this purpose.

From the main navigation bar, select the "Invite" link. This will bring you to the menu as displayed below.

> » show my invite link
> » view past invites
> » Help

**myspace.com**
a place for friends

to: (email addresses)

(separate multiple addresses by commas)

your message here: (optional)

(max 250 characters, no HTML)

Send Invite

### The MySpace Invite interface

It's simple to invite your friends. Add their email addresses in to the top box, and separate them with commas.

In the message box, you can add a customized message in order to encourage them to sign up.

Many web sites are notorious for using imported contact lists to mass mail web users under the guise of the person that just signed up. If you want your message to be seen as more than just spam, it's absolutely vital that you customize your message.

You can only use a maximum of 250 characters, but that should be enough to get your point across. Keep it short when asking your friends if they'll sign up and offer their support.

Use the invite system to create personalized invitations. Most people appreciate an email that means something instead of a generic email that everyone receives. While this will take more time, it is worth doing in order to cultivate an invested friends list. You're not simply trying to amass the most friends, you're building your audience one fan at a time.

Your MySpace profile is your window to the world. It might only receive a fleeting glance from the passers-by, so grabbing their attention is important. We'll be looking at how you can create a catchy profile later, but it's equally important to have relevant information on the page. This is why the profile fields are so important.

| Upcoming Shows | Band Details | Basic Info | Manage Songs | Listing Info |
|---|---|---|---|---|

Headline: _____
(Edit)

Bio _____
(Edit)

Members _____
(Edit)

Influences _____
(Edit)

Sounds Like: _____
(Edit)

Website _____
(Edit)

Record Label: unsigned
(Edit)

Label Type: Unsigned
(Edit)

*The MySpace band profile editing screen*

To modify your profile, select the "Edit Profile" link from the account management screen. You will be taken to the menu shown above.

This is where you can customize the information displayed to the public.

- **Headline**

    Your headline is important. It's one of the first things the user will notice, as it's positioned directly next to your picture. Your headline can serve several purposes.

    - Promotion of a new album or tour (e.g. Our New Single – Out March 30th). Use the headline to promote your upcoming work. If you're planning on releasing a single for download, mark it up in your Headline with a release date. This will instantly let the reader know what you're up to.

    - A catchy slogan that fits in with the genre you're appealing to. If you can think of a catchy slogan, it's a useful marketing mechanism. Having a catchphrase or gimmick can help establish your brand. The punk bands of the '70s and '80s made a lot of money using slogans and t-shirt-friendly phrases. It was part of their appeal, and people like to buy into something that seems cool.

    - A simple description of the band and its sound

- **Bio**

  This field allows you to write a short history of your band or act. MySpace users have a short attention span. If you blitz them with an essay, they'll avoid it completely. Limit your bio to a couple of paragraphs of short and snappy text. Leave a link to an extended version if you must, but don't let it clog up your page.

- **Members**

  If you're a band, list each member.

- **Influences**

  Reel off bands and artists that have inspired you. It might seem more like homage to other people's work rather than announcing your own, but it can actually be enormously helpful. For example, if one artist is inspired by Elvis and another is inspired by Pink Floyd, more often than not you can get a pretty good idea of how that act is likely to sound.

- **Sounds Like**

  This box lets you state what your music resembles most in sound and spirit. It's important to offer an accurate comparison because people will search out new acts based on what they sound like. Many people have used a web site such as Last. FM or Mercora where it's possible to find new artists based on who sounds similar. MySpace is exactly the same. Searches are carried out and if you meet the criteria, your music will be suggested. Don't lie about your sound. It's not a good idea to pretend that you sound like a famous act if in fact you don't. Look for other lesser-known artists in the same boat as yourself. It's likely that fans of these artists are going to be more open-minded about listening to your own work. Don't be afraid to say that you sound like an act which not many people have heard of. Honesty is the best policy.

- **Web site**

  If you have an official web site, place the URL here.

- **Record Label**

  Another opportunity to promote your record label.

- **Label Type**

  Once again, you'll be able to choose between Major, Indie and Unsigned.

# A DOMAIN TO IMPROVE YOUR IMAGE

It's possible to be successful on MySpace without ever having to purchase a Dot Com domain. But that doesn't stop people from investing in them. As you will learn later, there are many advantages of having a music web site devoted to your career and upcoming gigs.

Several reasons to consider a domain:

- **They look professional**

  People respond more positively to non-subbed domains like MyBand.com rather than AnotherWebsite.com/MyBand. By having your own domain, you're showing that you're in charge of your own site. By taking the prefix of another web site, you're revealing your dependence on their service. Of course, it isn't going to matter when the user gets to the web site. But first impressions are important. By having an identifiable domain, you can focus on your marketing campaign with greater precision. A professional URL looks much better on a business card than a MySpace sub domain.

- **They're easier to remember**

  People are easily confused when they have to remember extended URLs from across the web. A simplified URL is much easier to save in the memory bank, even if it deviates slightly from the actual username that you're using on MySpace. People are more likely to remember a Dot Com domain. It doesn't have to be a Dot Com either. Dot NET, Dot ORG, Dot TV and Dot CO UK are all good choices.

- **Ease of change**

  You also have to consider a scenario where for whatever reason you need to open up a new MySpace account with a different URL. If you've spent hundreds of dollars on the promotion of your old URL, that money will be disappearing in to the gutter. If you have a registered domain, you can change the name servers and settings to point to your new page without losing a single visitor along the way.

# THE DEFAULT MYSPACE PROFILE

It might not look particularly spectacular, but the default MySpace profile is an excellent starting point for your page.

You don't HAVE to use fancy designs to grab the user's attention, no matter how many millions of members choose to do so.

As you can see in the screenshot on the next page, the standard profile is simple and clean with a white background.

The general information is clearly marked and you don't have to worry about poorly contrived color schemes getting in the way of essential information.

There are two ways that you can look at the use of the default profile layout. While it can be seen as an uninspiring and rather bland template, it could also be considered an effective presentation which leaves the user to focus on the thing that matters most – your music.

*The default MySpace page layout*

# THIRD PARTY PROFILE GENERATORS

With the booming success of MySpace, many third parties have been created that allow you to customize, enhance, and personalize your profile. A simple Google search of "MySpace" will return thousands of results, many of them external web sites dedicated solely to users who want to add a little extra to their profiles.

Some web sites offer code snippets and custom media players. Others offer fully-fledged MySpace layouts.

One of the most popular tools is the profile generator.

Web developers have worked tirelessly to produce applets that include HTML and CSS (Cascading Style Sheet) code that can be slotted into your profile.

The code turns the default page into something remarkably different. If you're wondering where those profile designs are coming from, it's all in the code.

You can search around the web and get a ready-made profile layout. But you should ask yourself if you really want to be sharing the same designer layout as somebody else.

Design web sites are frequented a lot these days so you could be using a profile shared by HUNDREDS of other users.

Another option you can use is the set of generator tools that allow you to customize the basics of your profile and completely overhaul the generic look. Below are some of the items you can change on your profile page:

- Background color
- Background image
- Font
- Table colors
- Style, size and colors of the page border
- Style of the scrollbar
- Display order (whether to flip the display picture to the right-hand side)
- Opacity

The options are many. The best part is that you don't have to know a single line of HTML and CSS code. The generator tools enable you to see how your profile will look as you build it. Once you're happy, simply copy and paste the pre-generated code.

You will need to paste the code somewhere in your profile—usually the Biography or About Me field.

Third party generators usually only ask that you include a return link to their site on your profile page.

When you generate the code for your profile, the host web site will place a return link. You won't see it, but when your profile loads, there will normally be an image link from the web site where you generated the code. Probably something along the lines of "This profile was designed by… Get your own today!"

For typical MySpace users, this is fine. But for bands and artists trying to look professional, it can detract from your image depending on how tastefully it's done.

As of this writing, it appears that MySpace is also going to add features that will allow you change many of these items as well via "Edit Profile."

Bonus Chapters A and B of this book include various codes that you can use to customize your profile page, and make it look more unique.

## HOW MUCH IS TOO MUCH?

When you are designing your profile page, bear in mind that a few changes are all you need to differentiate yourself from others. If you add too many colors, fonts, and other visual devices, you will distract from the music you are promoting.

**Stop!**

There is such a thing as too much decoration, and unfortunately, many MySpace users do not know when to stop.

When decorating your profile page, keep the following in mind:

- Remember why you registered in the first place.

- Don't lose sight of your goals. The focal point of your profile should always be the small MySpace media application that plays the music. Tampering with this principle is a waste of time.

- Put yourself in the shoes of the web user who's stumbled upon your profile. Are they that interested in fancy colors and impressive images?

- A nice color scheme with some well-placed opacity tricks can do wonders for a profile. Simplicity is the best design strategy.

- Keep colors fairly neutral with plain shades rather than audacious bright lime greens or electric blues. For most people, loud colors are a distraction.

One of the best ways to know whether you've got too much happening on your profile is to look around and see what other popular artists are doing. Do their pages look similar? Have they received any comments about having a "cool profile?"

Get to know your target audience and work out what they like. Design a profile page that is eye-catching, but easy to use.

## HIRING A DESIGNER

If you're not keen on the prospect of using a ready-made profile template and you can't achieve the desired effect with a generator, there is another option.

Hiring a freelance template designer to build your profile page will save you time so you can focus on other aspects of your career.

Assuming you can afford to pay a designer, you'll be able to describe exactly what you want your profile to look like. As long as you choose a good designer, you should be left with a template that looks unique without sacrificing functionality.

You won't see other profiles cropping up with the same layout, and when users view your profile, it should seem fresh. A good first impression is important.

So what can you expect to pay for a design? There's a lot of competition on the market and you'll ultimately be the one to benefit from this.

There are several freelance auction web sites you can visit on the Internet. It's worth checking the three main freelance web sites below to get an estimate.

- *http://www.guru.com*

- *http://www.elance.com*

- *http://www.getafreelancer.com*

You can also post an open job to see the types of responses you receive. Make sure you review their portfolio and weigh any additional factors—such as time to complete the project.

If you do decide to hire a professional designer, make sure you provide a thorough explanation of what you expect from them. Express what your goals are. You want a cool looking site but your primary objective is getting people to listen.

Finally, test the design before you pay for it. Confirm that it works. Try a multitude of different profile combinations to ensure that it is working correctly.

## USING MYSPACE SEO FOR TRAFFIC

Many Internet Marketing experts rely heavily on Search Engine Optimization (SEO) as a way of directing traffic to a web site.

SEO can be used in a variety of ways that can help boost your web presence.

If you run a search on Google, the top ten or twelve web sites will be returned on the first page, while others will be buried under hundreds of results. The rankings are determined by a search engine algorithm. Nobody outside of Google HQ can claim to know the exact calculations of the algorithm, but we can predict some of the most important factors.

Of these factors, keyword usage is one of the most important.

By designing a MySpace profile with optimized content, it is possible to dramatically improve our search engine listings because most people seek out their favourite bands by making use of the search function.

For example, say your work sounds similar to the music of Ciara.

It's possible to target Ciara's fans by optimizing your profile with keywords her fans would use.

For example, plugging her album names into your musical influences box, you have a shot at catching some of the traffic from web users searching for those particular records. While not all of Ciara's fans will click on your profile, some may be curious enough to listen to one of your songs.

Here's another strategy using the profile fields on your page to optimise the likelihood of your URL being returned on search pages.

Consider recording a cover of a song from an artist who is popular in the genre that you're focusing on. If you sound like Ciara, why not record one of her songs and upload it to your music player? It's likely that you'll draw hits from Ciara fans who might simply want to know whether you've done a faithful job of reproducing her work. If they like it, there's a good chance they'll stick around to check out some of your original material.

The cover song will be returned in searches for the original version. This is how many artists get coverage on MySpace.

Not only will it affect your MySpace search listings, but it will improve your search ranking on sites such as Google, Yahoo and MSN too. Use these techniques on other social networking sites as well.

## HELPFUL TIPS ON IMPROVING YOUR MYSPACE PAGE

Throughout this chapter, you have learned how to create a MySpace profile. In bonus chapters A and B, you will find coding you can use to personalize your profile page.

Listed below are simple tips that will allow you to personalize your page and attract more attention without having to alter the current code:

- Using a picture that is taller rather than wider will make your profile stand out more when you are added to a friends list.

- Changing your URL on your profile page is helpful for a few reasons. Choosing a name that is easy to remember will help fans and others find your page. Adding a keyword or two will help search engines find your profile, which will result in higher rankings.

- Keep in mind that once you choose your MySpace URL, you won't be able to change it, so choose something that makes sense.

- Adding a logo is a good way to create name recognition on MySpace.

- Link your MySpace page to your web site and vice versa. This will help increase your web exposure. Include keywords into your link which will also be picked up by search engines.

- Add high PR rating Google profile pages to your friends list in order to improve your own web ranking. Google's PR rating represents how important the page is on the web. It assumes that if one page links to another, it is giving an endorsement and a vote for the other site. This can be done by searching for the highest ranking profiles using the advanced search feature on Google. Enter the search term "MySpace profiles" and for the domain enter "MySpace.com" so it will narrow your search to only those profiles on MySpace with the highest rankings. Simply do a friend request and when approved send them a comment. This is a very advantageous strategy!

- If you want to add more names to your friends list, placing a "Add Me" button in a comment on a popular profile with a large friends list is a powerful way to get a large amount of new friends. You can use any picture you want to draw attention, and when a new friend clicks on it they will be asked to accept you as a friend. In bonus chapter A, you will find the code needed to create one of these buttons.

- Podcasting from your blog or MySpace page is a good way to increase your fan base. A podcast is exactly the same as a blog, but with audio as well. To create a podcast, you need to upload your songs or other audio content to your web site or you can host your podcast for free at http://www.podomatic.com/ You can then add your podcast to your MySpace blog or page by pasting in your podcast URL. We'll go into more detail later in this book in the podcasting section.

These tips can help you gain more exposure on the Internet and increase your friend list and search engine ranking.

Chapter 5
# ▸ Introducing Your Work

It's time to upload your songs and video. Your musical work is the corner-stone of your profile. It's critical that you upload only your best songs.

## THE MYSPACE MUSIC PLAYER

This is the application that enables users to listen to songs in an artist's profile.

*fig. 13 MySpace Music Player*

It's easy to use and comes with several useful features. Besides the standard media buttons, there are links underneath each song.

- **Download**

    Allows users to download your song

- **Rate**

    Allows visitors to rate your song. These ratings are recorded and used to determine positions in the MySpace charts. You should allow your songs to be rated on any social networking site you belong to. Ratings influence your overall popularity on the sites and are useful feedback. A high position in the charts equates to a much greater likelihood of front page exposure.

- **Comments**

    Allows visitors to comment on your song.

- **Lyrics**

    Users will be able to read the lyrics of your songs.

- **Add**

    This function is unique to MySpace. Every user can add a single song to their profile. By clicking the Add link, the song is automatically placed on the user's page.

Use this feature. Encourage people to add your song to their profile page. This will help circulate your band name throughout the site and encourage music producers and labels to check out your profile page. If they notice your band name popping up on various profile pages they will stop and listen to your songs.

Since MySpace is a competitive networking site, you must do whatever it takes to get noticed. Mention adding your songs to fans through your blog, forums, and in emails you send.

The MySpace Music Player is designed to work across all of the major web browser platforms. It's designed with universal users in mind so you shouldn't face too many problems.

## ADDING A SONG

Adding songs to the MySpace Player is easy.

Log in to your account and navigate to the account management screen where the main options are listed. Select "Edit Profile."

You'll now see the basic profile menus, along with a tab marked "Manage Songs." Click on this tab and you'll find yourself viewing another menu. It will look like the screenshot below.

Three options apply to the settings of your songs.

**Page Settings**

☐ Allow users to add songs to their profile

☑ Auto-play first song when someone views my profile

☐ Check this box to randomize song play. If the box is left unchecked, your first song will play.

**Update Settings**

*fig. 14 standard MySpace song settings*

The first option gives fans the option of adding songs to their profile pages.

I strongly recommended that you enable this option as it will have an effect on your overall MySpace ranking, as I said before. If people like what they hear and add it to their own profiles, your music is going to be heard by their friends and anybody who happens to land on their page.

"Auto-play first song when someone views my profile," is another option I recommend. Enabling this means that the user doesn't have to press the play button for your music to be heard.

Some MySpace users don't want to have music blasted through their ears unexpectedly. But they have the option to overrule your selection and prevent music being directly streamed if they so choose.

Checking this box is way to get visitors to stop and listen to your music. Because most people are attracted to visual images, they may not be impressed with your profile page design choices and move on without listening to your music. With so many profile pages to look at, this is human nature.

Get people interested in your music right away and they will stay and listen to your songs. Choose a song that is representative of your music as this will give people a good idea of the type of music your band performs.

The final option merely serves to randomize the song that will play in your profile, if you have more than one added.

Be careful in selecting this. Do you have one particular song which conveys your work in the right way for first time listeners? Or do you have a new single coming out which you want to focus attention on?

If the answer to either question is yes, I'd suggest you leave this box unchecked. It makes sense to promote the work that suits your current needs.

Of course, if you have the luxury of an expansive repertoire and no immediate commitments, plugging the randomize feature and hoping people come back to hear more than one song is a good idea.

Once you're happy, click "Update Settings."

To reach the menu for adding new songs, go to your account management page.

Click "Edit Profile" and then "Manage Songs."

Above the next menu shown, you'll find a link titled "Add Song." Click this and you'll be presented with the options shown on the next page.

⚠ **Warning: MySpace terms of use prohibit uploading or posting copyrighted content belonging to others without permission. Repeated uploading of copyrighted content belonging to others can result in the termination of membership privileges.**

**Edit Song Details**

**Edit Song Information**

| | |
|---|---|
| Song Name: | |
| Album Name: | |
| Album Year: | |
| Record Label: | |
| Lyrics: | |

☐ Allow users to rank this song [more info]

☐ Allow users to download this song [more info]

| Update | Cancel |

*The Add Song Screen*

Here's how you should fill it in.

- **Song Name**

  The title of the song you're about to add.

- **Album Name**

  The album that the song comes from, if any.

- **Album Year**

  The release year for the album – not the current date.

- **Record Label**

  The record label that the song was released on, if any.

- **Lyrics**

   If you choose to provide lyrics, they'll be visible to users from the relevant link in the MySpace Music Player. Making the lyrics available to visitors is a way to get those who prefer visual images to stay and listen to your songs. Reading the lyrics as they are listening to your songs serves as reinforcement and cause them to remember your band after listening to other bands on MySpace, even those with a sound that is similar to yours. A lot of musicians forget to use all the tools available on MySpace, which is a shame because they are missing some wonderful marketing opportunities.

- **Allow Users to Rank This Song**

   Check this box to allow song ratings. This is a good selection for improving your ranking in the MySpace charts even if the rating is a poor one. Any publicity is good publicity. Visitors may stop to see why others gave your songs a poor ranking. They may also leave some good comments that challenge the previous ranking. This is a good way to use visitor opinion as a marketing tool. You can ask visitors on your profile page to rank your song in order to take sides. You are going to get a mix of good and bad ratings anyway, so why not make a game of it and increase the number of visitors that visit your site and build your friends list at the same time?

- **Allow Users to Download This Song**

   It's a risky move to leave this selected. Do you really want to provide freebies? You'll have a great deal of difficulty attracting the major labels if you've been giving your premium songs away. If it's an unwanted B-side, by all means, make it a download. Just be careful not to give away a potential number one hit. One exception would be if you simply want to get loyal fans who will come to your performances and build up a huge fan base. In this case, you hope to make a return from the shows and possibly merchandise, as well as creating a buzz.

Once you've filled in your details, click "Update."

You'll now have the chance to upload the song itself.

Make sure you pick the right file, and wait for the upload tool to complete. Be patient. Depending on your connection speed, it can take several minutes to finish uploading a track.

Once the song is uploaded, you'll receive a confirmation message and that's that.

Congratulations! You've just added your first track to the MySpace Music Player.

# USING A THIRD PARTY MEDIA APPLET

Third media applets are used by musicians who want to upload more than four songs at a time on their MySpace profile page. If you have a web site, you can easily link it to your profile page and not have to worry about installing a third media applet.

But if you want to include more than six songs and your web site is not complete yet, third party media players are readily available on the Internet. You can upload your songs to a separate server and embed the player in your profile.

Some of them look snazzy; some of them look like they've been designed by people who really shouldn't have access to computers. Find one that is easy to use and fits the overall image you are trying to convey to visitors.

There are drawbacks to using a third party media applet on your profile page, however. While you can upload more than six songs, you may be missing out on some great marketing tools offered by MySpace. Reasons to avoid adding a media player to your profile page include:

- **Users can't add songs from third party players**

- **Users can't rate songs from third party players**

    This is another marketing tool you will not be able to use. I can't stress enough the importance of using the tools provided for free by MySpace. By limiting the use of these tools, your profile page will be lost among many pages on the site.

- **Users aren't going to stick around to listen to your collection**

    While you may want to add more songs to your profile page, carefully consider the marketing opportunities lost. Ask youself if it is more important to become well known on MySpace with Six songs than upload an entire album that many will never know about?

People rarely stay on the same profile for longer than it takes to listen to a couple of songs even if you have many songs to offer.

While it may be rewarding to upload all the songs you have ever recorded, the bottom line if that MySpace is a social network, not a music store. It looks as if MySpace will allow you to sell your music in the near future, however. If you have an album you want to sell, visit sites like CDBaby and sell it there. Or put it online into iTunes etc by using a aggregator like IODA or Tunecore. You can let visitors know the music is available by advertising it on your profile page.

Keep in mind that visitors on MySpace want to sample your music, not spend an hour or more listening to it. Since there are many musicians that visitors want to check out while they are on MySpace, you will have to show them your best work in a short amount of time. Adding extra songs is not going to make a huge difference in your success.

# CHOOSING THE RIGHT MATERIAL

For many aspiring artists, the songs chosen represent the best they have to offer. But not everyone has a large number of strong songs to choose from.

If this is the case, I recommend you showcase your best song and upload the others at a later date. Let this song be the one that people hear when they visit your page. Over time, you will record more songs that you can rotate on your profile page. Remember that MySpace is only one of several social networking sites you should be active on. While MySpace is the largest site, it should be used along with other sites in order to give you the most exposure online.

When choosing a song, choose the one that best represents you and your music, or that gets the best reaction at your performances or from friends and fans that have taken a listen. Does one of your songs stand out more than the rest? Focus on the song that has the strongest appeal.

The best song to have sitting at the top of your playlist is the song that makes the most immediate impression. This means that it touches people in a way that your other songs do not.

It's also important to make sure your second song is just as good. If you hook the listener, get them intrigued, and then produce a follow-up song that blows them away—you're pulling in an upward direction.

While you have six spaces for songs, you don't have to use all six. I recommend that you try to fill each slot with a song only if to increase your ranking and exposure to fans on MySpace.

As discussed in previous chapters, record a cover of another artist's song and use keywords to get people to your page. Use a slot for a live performance or tribute to another famous musician.

Another strategy for showcasing your music is to use compilation tracks.

Have you ever seen the short advertisements during television breaks that promote a new album? These are essentially thirty-second tracks that feature small samplings of your songs.

The downside is that they don't get to hear the whole songs.

If you are going to use a compilation package, you can include one full track plus the snippets. That way, the compilation simply acts as an incentive to search out more of your work.

Always think carefully before you choose the songs for your MySpace profile, and don't underestimate the importance of ordering them properly.

If you look at other profiles, you'll find that the top song is by far the most listened to. Don't be fooled by this. The true mark of a popular sound is in the difference between the number of listeners on the first song, and the number of listeners on the second. If you can keep them listening, you're doing something right.

# VIDEO APPEAL

In additional to your songs, a video is an excellent way to connect with your fans on a completely different level. It can do wonders for your brand recognition and it can spruce up your MySpace profile too. I strongly recommend that you upload only GOOD videos you happen to have in your possession. Not only do they show the MySpace browser what you're really about, but a quality video is one that people will want to feature on their web sites, profile pages, and other sites. The exposure is brilliant and not only do people learn about your sound, but they'll recognize your face too.

Videos don't have to be of the MTV variety. There are many different forms they can take.

If you've taken the time to record a standard video for one of your songs, there's no point in leaving it hidden away. It should be uploaded and added to your profile without hesitation.

What about live performances and footage from gigs? Do you have any clips of your band in action? What about a live acoustic version of your most popular track? Behind the scenes?

Gig footage is always a popular choice for MySpace videos.

There is a massive demand for enjoyable videos. People will spend hours at a time browsing through footage and spreading word of their favorites.

You don't have to include songs at all.

It's possible to send out an excellent image of power and importance by uploading an interview. Even if you have to get a friend to conduct the interview for you, it's possible to raise your profile by sharing your opinions and insights with the rest of the MySpace community.

By showing visitors that you want to take the time to talk about your passions, they will listen to your songs in order to learn more about you. As long as the interview is conducted professionally and offers some real insight, then you will increase your fan base quickly.

Another idea is to upload your video in installments and let people know when the next instalment will air. Use your MySpace calendar to specify dates and times. People who want to know more will tune in.

Showing a fun and likeable persona is an excellent marketing asset that can be showcased better through video than through the music alone. Here's how to upload a video into your MySpace.

Go to the main account management screen.

From the homepage, select the "Add / Change Videos" link. This will bring you to a whole new menu, from which you can interact with the video sharing community.

Select the "Upload" tab and you'll see a screen that resembles the one on this page.

| | |
|---|---|
| **Title:** | |
| | Maximum length: 64 |
| **Description:** | |
| | Maximum length: 3000. Characters remaining: 3000. |
| **Tags:** | |
| | Tags are keywords associated with your video. Separate tags with spaces. For example: Tom snowboard face plant |

**Categories**

**Video Categories:** Select 1-3

☐ Animals      ☐ Schools and Education
☐ Animation/CGI      ☐ Science and Technology
☐ Automotive      ☐ Sports
☐ Comedy and Humor      ☐ Travel and Vacations
☐ Entertainment      ☐ Video Games
☐ Extreme Videos      ☐ VideoBlogging
☐ Instructional      ☐ Weird Stuff
☐ Music
☐ News and Politics

**Visibility:** ⊙ Public Your video will appear in search results and category lists
           ○ Private Your video will not appear in search results and category lists.

☐ I agree to the MySpace **Terms and Conditions**

Continue

*The Video Upload menu*

- **Title**

   The title of your video can be a maximum of 64 characters.

- **Description**

   It's a good idea to use the description box to offer a little extra information about your work. If somebody watches the video and likes what they see, it does no harm in telling them a little more about yourself. They might search out more of your work. Use keywords in your description so your video will be featured not only in the MySpace search engines, but on Google as well. Later in this book, I will explain the importance of keywords and how they can be used to increase web ranking and exposure on the Internet. If you have a web site, also include the URL so visitors will be able to find it easier.

- **Tags**

  Tags operate as search terms for your video. They're extremely important if you hope to be found in the video sharing community. If your tags are so obscure that nobody will search for them, you can forget about reaping search traffic. It's a good idea to use the words that are relevant to your genre. A lot of people search for funny videos so wise use of "comedy" and "humor" tags are recommended. Tags are similar to keywords, so be sure to take advantage of them.

- **Categories**

  You can pick up to three categories for your video. It will be listed under each category so choosing the right one is important. Check the boxes that apply to your video.

- **Visibility**

  Always set your video access levels to "Public." Allowing public access means that you'll be listed in the search results, and also in the categories of your choice.

Finally, you must agree to the MySpace Terms and Conditions, and check the box. Click the "Continue" button and you'll be taken to the upload form.

Locate the video on your computer and continue. MySpace will then transfer the video from your personal computer on to the MySpace servers. It can take a while, even longer than songs. Videos tend to be large files. Depending on your Internet Connection, it could take up to 30 minutes to complete the upload.

You will receive a confirmation message when the server has received the video file. Your video will be approved and other MySpace users will be able to access it.

Don't stop there, though. Upload your video to YouTube and the other major video hosts too. Marketing should make use of all possible avenues.

# Chapter 6
## ▸ Social Networking On MySpace

Now that you have a completed MySpace profile, it's time to look at how to interact on the MySpace network. This is very important because the amount of time you spend marketing your music will determine how popular you become on MySpace.

MySpace marketing is all about getting your name out there and making "friends." While you shouldn't expect this to extend to real life, a "MySpace friend" is a friend to appreciate. Every user you can get on your friend list will show others that your page is worth exploring.

You shouldn't be concerned with the personalities of the people on your friend's list. A friend is a friend and in the world of MySpace, the more you have, the better you'll be received.

Did you know that some MySpace profile lists have sold for up to $25,000? That's an incredible sum of money for something which is absolutely free, but for those who don't take the time to market themselves on MySpace, buying lists may be the best they can do. With the tips learned in this book, you will never have to buy friend lists. Simply connecting with people, being friendly, and offering great music is all you will need to do.

While some are willing to pay to tap into the enormous resources that a well developed profile can bring, sending a bulletin to thousands of willing readers is extremely profitable and costs much less. There's a difference between sending messages to random friends and sending them to people who are targeted for the purpose of what you're trying to sell. Learning these differences and taking advantage of them will help you gain more friends and increase your exposure.

Social networking is a rewarding game to play, especially if you're good at it.

## YOU'VE GOT FRIENDS. USE THEM!

There's a network of over 100 million MySpace users just waiting to learn more about your music. So should you spend your time trying to recruit friends you already know in real life?

The answer is that they will take less convincing than strangers to join your list. If you have twenty or thirty friends and family on your list, it will be much easier to get strangers to join.

Never underestimate what the people around you can do to help your cause. Marketing can be a tricky business when you are first starting out. Sometimes the best way to succeed is to get your friends to do the initial talking for you.

Creating a viral buzz is something that will make a difference in how successful you become as a musician when marketing yourself online. It's possible to generate a buzz without using your friends, but why not ask them to join? It's a great way to support your career and it costs nothing to join.

Work systematically through your contacts. Find your friends and nudge them in the direction of your MySpace profile. Ask them to join and add you to their account. Encourage them to leave positive comments and high ratings on your songs. Ask them to feature you in their top ten friends.

I'm not suggesting you spend all of your free time promoting your MySpace campaign, but it doesn't do any harm in using what is available to help you succeed. Remember that marketing your music is an ongoing process.

Open your eyes to marketing opportunities and accept that you probably won't see the effects of Internet marketing immediately. It can take time for your name to catch on. The important thing is that you keep pushing your name, especially around friends. Don't stop there, either! Speak to the friends of your friends—and their family too!

## THE "FRIEND" TRAIN

There are many web sites that focus on offering an "Advertise and be Advertised" strategy for those looking to rack up new friends with minimal work. These are called "Friend Trains."

These trains will require you to sign up with a unique ID on a third party web site. You will be given a code to post as a bulletin to officially "jump on the train."

When you post the bulletin, you'll be advertising another member of the train. It's like an immense chain of people using the same system. And of course, the third party site will detect that you've posted the bulletin.

You'll then be moved forward in the queue and when other people sign up to the web site they'll be posting bulletins with you as the subject. These bulletins will go out to hundreds of friends—depending on how many the user has added.

The one requirement is that you do have at least some friends added to your list. After all, the idea is that you're advertising the person before you on the train. If you're posting bulletins for only yourself to read, the train will not be successful.

Friend trains can be a good way to generate exposure and get friends quickly so others will see that you have an active list, but it's hard to know what to expect. You could be lucky and receive promotion from a member with thousands of friends, or you could draw the short straw.

The good news is that you can jump back on the train whenever you want. This means that you'll need to post another bulletin, but the rewards are obvious. It's a good marketing shortcut even though the results will vary. Just do a search for "MySpace Friend Trains" and you'll find plenty to choose from.

It's a good idea to check with the service beforehand so you know what exactly you're going to be required to post in your bulletins. If the message is tacky and overly "robotic," you're likely to leave a negative impression on your current friends.

It's also worth noting that posting too many friend train bulletins may cause your other announcements to go unnoticed. Much like an email campaign, you should post bulletins a few times a month or during the year so those on your friends list don't consider you a spammer. In addition, friend trains might not give you targeted friends.

## PAYING FOR FRIENDS

I have provided a number of ways for you to make friends on MySpace without paying for them, but if you have limited time to spend online or don't want to spend time making these connections, there are web sites you can visit that sell friend lists. Depending on how much you have to spend, you may be able to jumpstart your friends list with a thousand names or more.

Be careful when paying for these services, however. They are risky and there is little chance you will receive your money back if it turns out to be a scam.

By using certain third party companies, you make a one-time payment and wait to see the results. Having received your money, the provider gets to work and serves up the friends that you asked for in about 24 hours.

For example, one service online offers 1,000 new friends at a cost of $10. Now when you consider how much work would go into attracting 1000 friends off your own back, $10 is a small cost. Say you're willing to pay $100 up front? What does that bring? It provides a whooping 10,000 friends to target with your bulletins and comments, and that's without the discounts that come with many of the plans.

While this may seem like a simple solution, make sure the web site you are using is legitimate before you proceed. In addition these friends will not necessarily be targeted friends.

# THE MESSAGING INTERFACE

With such a huge network of users, it would be foolish for MySpace not to implement a messaging system.

Thankfully, you'll find an efficient messaging system in place on the site. It isn't flashy and it doesn't have the many options that come with email clients – but for promoting your music, it is a good tool to have.

There are many reasons why you may want to message another user:

- It could be done as part of a dedicated viral promotion campaign.

- It could also be to strike up friends and acquaintances that might be of use to you in the future.

Of course, there are times when you won't initiate conversation at all. The nature of MySpace is such that any users can message each other at any time—providing they haven't been blocked.

MySpace is configured by default so that you'll receive an email alert when a new message is received. This is ideal for building a fan base by answering questions quickly instead of letting them pile up over time.

The interface is easy to use and you can see an illustration of the layout below.

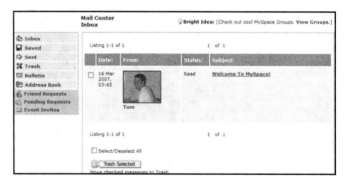

*The MySpace messaging interface*

As you can see, the screen is divided in to a navigation pane and the inbox itself. The message from Tom is one that every new user receives when they register.

- **Inbox**

  This is the screen above. Any new messages will be flagged with a status of "Unread." Once you've opened a mail, it'll turn to "Read." If you send a reply, the status will change to "Replied."

- **Saved**

  Any messages that you don't want to lose can be added to the "Saved" folder. These will be easy to find as they're accessible via the link in the navigation.

- **Sent**

  When you send a message, a copy will be stored in this folder along with the status. You can check to see whether the message has been read. If you're operating a messaging marketing campaign, the status can be a good indicator of how successful your pitch is. Messages that are read and tossed aside could potentially be revised.

- **Trash**

  For all of the messages you don't want to keep.

- **Bulletin**

  The messaging system is closely interlinked with the bulletin system. They both make use of the messaging interface. Clicking the bulletin link will take you to the latest bulletins.

- **Address Book**

  If you want to keep track of your contacts, they can be added to the address book for future reference. If you're marketing to a large number of users and receiving lots of replies, it's a good idea to keep track of who is who so you can send a unique response.

One way to separate your page from the rest is by adding personal touches to your marketing campaigns. Much like getting flyers and other non-personal junk in the mail, sending generic messages to message inboxes will be trashed.

Storing the addresses of those who have a lot of friends on their own profile page is a great way to reach more people when sending out bulletins. One of the great things about viral marketing is that your bulletins and other information will be sent to people on other friend lists. Maintaining a healthy list of email addresses will increase your own popularity.

- **Friend Requests**

  When users send you a friend request, you'll receive an approval message in this particular folder. You can accept or deny their request

  Always accept invitations to be on other people's friend lists. This is easy to follow and will increase your exposure on MySpace.

- **Pending Requests**

  Any unanswered friends requests submitted through your own account will be stored here.

- **Event Invites**

     Finally, if you receive any invitations to special events, they'll be listed here along with an option to mark yourself as in or out.

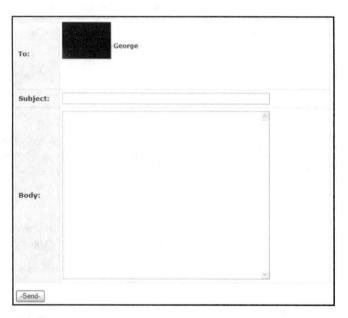

*The Send Message screen*

To send a message to another user, go to their profile and select the "Send Message" option from the user panel.

Remember that some users decide to skin their profiles using confusing colors and images. The "Send Message" link is often hidden under a strange icon. You can find it by holding your mouse over the icons until the relevant caption pops up.

As a musician trying to promote your music, you should not hide any functions under unfamiliar icons. If people have to search on your profile page for too long, they will leave and you will miss out on marketing opportunities.

Once you reach the screen to send messages, you'll see the username of the recipient along with their display picture.

In the previous screenshot, I've blacked out the user's display picture.

What you write in the subject will determine whether your message will be opened or not. Many people will not open anything that sounds like spam. Mention your band in your subject line so people will know you are a MySpace user and not an autoresponder.

Some people choose to use overtly professional titles which a user flags as spam before they've even opened.

While you may be able to get away with "Hi" or "Hey" for a little while, many spammers are now using these greetings to get people to open up their messages. While you want to appear friendly, you also want your messages to be opened and read by many people.

The idea of disguising yourself as a friend so that users open your mail without the pretences of spam and manufactured words is good as long as you let people know who you are. If you have the time to sift through their details, refer to them by name and mention your band's name. This will help people decide if they want to open your message or not.

The body of the mail is where you can place your message. Most users accept HTML in their mail. I'd like to point that over-dressing your emails can leave the user under the distinct impression that they're a recipient of a mass-marketing campaign, so make sure you "personalize" your correspondence in some small way. You can do this by:

- Mentioning their first name in your greeting

- Asking how their day is going

- Be specific about concert dates and other information without adding fluffy words or trying to get them to buy something

- End your message with a goodbye that you would normally use

There's nothing wrong with using the messaging system to inform people of your music, or to ask them to listen to your latest track. But remember that MySpace is primarily for social networking.

It's just plain rude to message them with a poorly disguised pitch and nothing else. Make use of humor whenever you can in order to make them read your entire message. It is very important to make it seem as if you're interested in what they have to say so they will want to visit your profile page, add you as a friend, or accept your invite to be a part of your friends list.

If you can encourage a reply, you can continue your sales pitch. We'll look at a way to do this with the assistance of automation software later.

The best way to provoke a reply, however, is to just ask questions. Questions don't have to be philosophical or testing. Just asking the user how they are doing will often catch them off-guard. If they're feeling chatty, they'll reply.

Remember that even though you might be sending many messages at a time, it's unlikely that the recipients will be receiving a flood of other messages. You are the focus of their attention for those few seconds when they open your mail. Make sure that you draw them into a friendly conversation as soon as possible.

Other tips to follow:

- Ask your questions BEFORE you plug your music. Make it seem as if you're interested in getting to know them, before serving your own purposes

- Keep an eye on the wording of your messages. It's often a good idea to word your messages slightly differently depending on the gender of the recipient

- If you're mailing a girl or guy, you might want to consider different lines of questions. Be sure to add a little humor and self-deprecation. It loosens their guard and makes them slightly more willing to give your work a listen

- Nobody likes an ego, so make sure the message isn't only about you. Focus on other topics in order to keep people interested in what you have to say

- Remember that you're asking for a favor. You can sugar coat the message all you want, but at the end of the day, you're still bargaining for the cooperation of the user

- Always remember to thank them, whether or not they decide to give their attention to your work. It's a good idea to add a small disclaimer apologizing in the event that you've wasted any of their time. Once again, this example of good online etiquette is absolutely crucial. You ARE looking for friends after all

## ATTENTION THROUGH BULLETINS

Sending bulletins is a great way of keeping your existing friends aware of any developments in your work.

Every user has a bulletin update area on their account management screen. Whenever a friend posts a bulletin, the subject will appear in this section.

| | |
|---|---|
| **To:** | Bulletins are messages that are sent to all your friends at the same time. |
| **Subject:** | |
| **Body:** | |

Post

### The Bulletin posting system

To access the screen to post new bulletins (above), go to your account management page. In the "My Mail" box, select the "Post Bulletin" option. This will bring you to the form above.

As you can see, the interface is similar to that of the messaging system. The only thing that changes is the recipient, which is no longer required.

When you post a bulletin, it will go out to the bulletin boxes of everybody in your friend's list. It's like a shared inbox.

You do have to bear in mind, however, that not everybody will be as inclined to open a bulletin. There are no bright red alerts to draw the user's attention to the message. The only item you have to catch attention with is the Subject field.

Your subject field – or title – will appear in the users' bulletin boxes.

Unlike the messaging utility, it's a good idea to think of something a little more intriguing than "Hello" or "Hi" for your subject.

The bulletin panel displays five links at a time. That leaves you with five times as much competition for the user's attention.

Use titles that are suggestive, but not quite revealing. If you can perk the user's interest, you're free to be as creative as you want.

People EXPECT bulletins to be impersonal. This makes them much better prospects for posters and graphic art than a private message. If you have a knack for producing high quality graphic design, this is the place to flaunt it on MySpace.

It makes sense that you'd use the bulletin system to keep fans updated, but it can be hard to balance the act of casually posting meaningful updates and blitzing people with more information than they can stand to read.

If you're struggling to think of reasons why you might want to use it, here are a few to consider:

- Let people know that you've uploaded a new song

- Announce a release date for new work or reveal cover art

- Provide details to upcoming events and reminders as the date draws near

- Announce that you've uploaded new photos

- Showcase a new blog, podcast or vlog (video blog)

- Announce a new video

There are things you should never post if you wish to maintain a professional image. These include:

- Desperate pleas for comments. People will leave them if they want to. Don't ask for them

- Constant reminders that tickets are still available for a show. If you make it sound like nobody is interested, you're not likely to get much of a response

- Useless surveys and quizzes

- Requests to add other users as friends. No matter how much people are willing to pay you, don't let yourself stoop to the level of promoting random strangers

A general rule, if you're posting more than one bulletin in any given day, you're posting too many.

## COMMENTING OTHER USERS

You've probably noticed by now that in your profile page, it's possible for other users to post comments about you.

You can control these via your account management options. It's possible to require that all comments are approved before reaching your profile. This lets you sift through and delete any harmful entries.

Leaving comments is a good way of staying in touch with your friends and it usually results in a returned comment.

You can either take a professional or personal approach. As far as comments are concerned, keep things casual and personal. People don't always take too kindly to their profiles being used as a marketing tool. That's not to say that you can't get away with a bit of undercover promotion however.

The main purpose of a comment is to get the user to click on your name and view your profile. It goes without saying that if you're going to leave one, you should ask a simple question which invites the recipient to return the gesture and access your page.

When they come back to your profile, there's a chance that they might listen to your music and spend a little longer than they originally intended.

The process is good for getting your name out there and keeping it there. It's better to be proactive and encourage communication than to sit there waiting for fans to come to you. With such high levels of competition, it's likely that you could be waiting for a long time unless you actively participate on the web site.

Be sure to leave plenty of comments on the profile pages of similar artists – preferably artists with a larger fan base than you. This will help to promote you and find the types of people that are interested in your work.

And don't forget to use the "Add Me" strategy discussed earlier in this book.

## ADDING AN UPCOMING SHOW

If you have a set of concert dates coming up, it makes sense to reveal these to your MySpace friends. MySpace provids you with a feature that automates the process of ordering and presenting your upcoming shows.

To get to the feature, access your normal MySpace homepage.

Click "Edit Profile." The page should open with a menu already tabbed to the correct screen. It will say "Add a New Show."

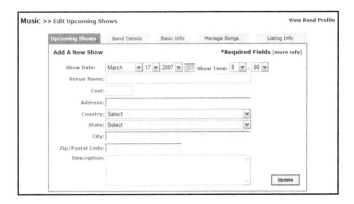

*The Edit Upcoming Shows screen*

As you can see, the Shows menu is designed to simplify the process of organizing a list of shows. It orders the events by date and presents them in a neat looking table. The shows will be accessible to MySpace users so they will know everything regarding your current activities.

I won't go through the details of the form as they're self-explanatory; however, remember to provide extensive details for how tickets can be purchased (presuming they're available), along with any other relevant details which might be of use to your fans.

The forum is another marketing tool to take advantage of. Given the vast array of options available to users, forums may seem a bit old fashioned, but use them, check them out to see what is on them.

The boards can be a great way of interacting with music fans. You can usually find plenty of healthy discussion. If you happen to be knowledge-able in your field, it's possible to earn a lot of respect by contributing valuable points to discussions.

If people appreciate your opinions, they're more inclined to visit your page. It's a win-win situation.

To use the forums, simply click the "Forum" link from the main MySpace navigation bar.

You'll see a huge list of boards, as seen on the next page:

| | | | |
|---|---|---|---|
| **Health & Fitness**<br>Work it in here; exchange tips, find a gym buddy. | Chat | 28830 | 433210 |
| **Love & Relationships**<br>Everyone's favorite topics, of course. | Chat | 69883 | 2408804 |
| **Movies**<br>Film buffs can buff here. Movie Reviews perhaps? | Chat | 8073 | 159786 |
| **Music**<br>Indie, mainstream and whatever suits your fancy. | Chat | 452372 | 5314789 |
| **MySpace**<br>Topics related to MySpace-- users, help, & general nonsense. | Chat | 524606 | 1548953 |
| **News & Politics**<br>War is mean politics. | Chat | 97427 | 2312443 |
| **Religion & Philosophy**<br>Let's be nice. Remember what Socrates said. | Chat | 54213 | 2242307 |
| **Science**<br>It's rumored that Carl Sagan actually created MySpace. | Chat | 7810 | 97283 |
| **Sports**<br>You got game b-baller? | Chat | 42703 | 734765 |
| **Television**<br>There is more to TV than the OC. | Chat | 29975 | 429983 |

*The Forum overview page*

As you can see by the posted statistics, the music forum is one of the busiest. You'll have to sift through a lot of simplified topics before finding one where your knowledge can be put to effective use. Of course, you don't have to take this approach.

If general music knowledge isn't your strong point, you can always make a few friends by being nice and offering a few comments on different forums. Forums have a reputation of attracting rude people, so a friendly face is always well received.

If you're going to post, make sure you believe what you say. It's not a good idea to follow trends in the hope of making friends.

It's easy to use the boards. Browse through the topics until you see something that perks your interest, then scroll to the bottom and you'll find the option to submit a reply.

You can also start topics of your own. This will give you more exposure and people will be referring to your first post in the topic. A few carefully generated topics and responses are a good way of getting your name spread around the boards in a hurry.

Generally, I recommend that you spend your time on the forums wisely. There isn't a HUGE scope for marketing opportunities, but making the occasional contribution can improve your brand recognition.

## USING CHAT ROOMS EFFECTIVELY

At the very bottom of the list of priorities are chat rooms.

You shouldn't have to use the chat rooms at all if that's not what you like to do. They're one of the least effective ways of marketing your music, primarily because they're so cluttered with useless spam. It can be hard to get your "Hello" noticed, let alone a sophisticated pitch.

But if you're absolutely insistent on making the most out of MySpace's features, here's how you would access the chat rooms.

Navigate to the MySpace homepage.

From here, you'll see links and images leading just about everywhere. Underneath the navigation bar, you should see a small panel looking something like the screenshot on the next page.

| | | | |
|---|---|---|---|
| Blogs | Classifieds | MySpaceIM | Schools NEW! |
| ChatRooms | Horoscopes | Music | Filmmakers NEW! |
| Events | Comedy | Videos | Jobs NEW! |

*The secondary navigation on the MySpace homepage.*

Clicking the "ChatRooms" link will bring you to the main chat menu. From here, it's possible to select your chat room of choice.

You can search out chat rooms with a number of filters.

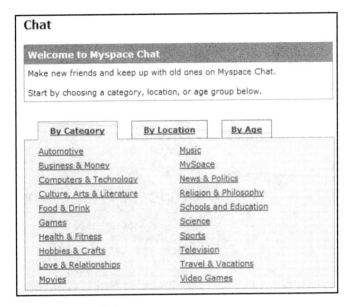

### The Chat Room choices

There are clearly many different chat rooms on the web site. For our purposes, the Music rooms are the best suited to the sort of people that you want to target.

There are two further tabs to consider. It's possible to enter rooms which focus on users from specific locations, or of specific age groups.

If you have a live show coming up in a certain location, it might be worth spreading the word in the chat room of that particular region. Don't expect incredible results, but you might be able to draw interest from two or three users. Maybe more if you're lucky.

Alternatively, if you're releasing work which is likely to appeal to fans of a certain era, you can enter the relevant age room. This is no guarantee. It's hard to say whether a certain group of people are going to like a particular genre based on their age alone. But you stand a better chance of appealing to Pink Floyd fans in an older room than, say, teenage chat.

So how should you go about promoting your music in the chat rooms? The best way is not to try to promote at all. Chat rooms are generally best used as a way of being friendly with people in the hope that they'll check out your page. It does happen sometimes, and you can increase your chances of success with a bit of undercover name-slipping.

Once you enter a room, it won't take long to see that there are many other users looking to promote their own products and services. This is another reason why direct advertising is unlikely to pay dividends.

In fact, the best way to appeal in such a fast-moving environment is to be yourself. If you've got a personality, now is the time to use it.

Forget about copy and pasting a pitch. Many users try this tactic, but it's against MySpace rules. A moderator will soon clean the mess and you'll find your reputation will be harmed.

It's also wise not to get involved in arguments. Trust me; they appear regularly in chat rooms. Make a pact with yourself when entering that you'll treat the room like the faceless entity that it is. There's nothing to gain by slinging verbal dirt at another user.

Just like forums, I'd recommend against relying too heavily on chat rooms. They don't return the greatest results, yet they can be some of the most time consuming marketing avenues on MySpace.

# MAKING THE MOST OF YOUR TIME

Marketing on MySpace can be a time consuming endeavor. If you take a hands-on approach to your campaign, hours can be whittled away tracing messages and following up comments.

For that reason, it's important that you learn how to make the most out of the time that you have—particularly when it comes to contacting MySpace members.

Efficiency is arguably the most important attribute to your campaign.

What good is it to contact 2,000 grunge or heavy metal fans if your music resembles rap or hip hop?

Even if you have as little as 30 minutes to spend marketing, it's possible to make an impression. You just have to use that time wisely. Send your messages and friend requests to the people that are most likely to enjoy your music.

The obvious way of ensuring this is to take advantage of similar bands friend lists. By this, I mean visiting their profiles and marking down the most active contributors. Make it your priority to contact the people who are most likely to find an interest in your work.

If you're dealing with severe time restraints, it's absolutely crucial that you use your time effectively. This means targeting the MySpace crowd and filtering out potential fans.

Another tactic that I'd recommend involves browsing the group categories. Look for communities that show an appreciation towards the work that you do.

For example:

- "Fans of hip hop"
- "80s Rock Appreciation Group"
- "Country music lovers"

Find a group that appreciates music similar to your own and sift through the registered members. You might not have hours at your disposal, but the time that you DO have will be spent contacting people with a mutual interest in your range of music.

## Chapter 7
# ▶ Creating a Music Web Site

A web site is a valuable tool to use when promoting your music. Not only can you upload songs, you can also write about your music and career, include an EPK (electronic promo kit), and sell your music if you choose.

## WEB SITE BASICS

When setting up your web site, it is important to focus on the following first:

- ISP (Internet service provider)
- Domain name
- Web host
- FTP client
- Web design

After you have chosen a domain name, found a web host, and chosen your web design, then you can focus on uploading songs, creating content, and much more. As you will see, a web site offers many ways to market to those on the Internet.

## ISP (INTERNET SERVICE PROVIDER)

An ISP is the company that provides you with an Internet connection. There are a few connections to choose from including cable, dial-up, and DSL. Since you will be uploading music on a regular basis to your MySpace page, Facebook, YouTube, and personal web site, I suggest you try to find the fastest ISP you can, which is usually cable.

Your cable company may offer package deals that include cable television and Internet at a discount. Check around to find the best deal. Most ISPs are no longer free and if they are, they usually limit the time you can spend online each month. This will hinder your marketing campaign, so choose an ISP that gives you plenty of freedom.

## DOMAIN NAME

The first step in creating your web site is to choose a domain name and register that name as soon as possible. Domain names are unique names given to your web site. They are included in URLs and are used to identify your site on search engines.

Registering your domain name is easy and it will protect you from others who might want to use it. You can register your domain name through web sites such as ivoy at http://www.ivoy.com - and countless others. You can also search through domain databases to see if a name is already taken, and possibly make an offer to purchase it if it is not available.

It is important to register your domain name each year so you can retain it for as long as you need it. You can register it for more than one year at the time of purchase as well with automatic renewals.

## WEB HOST

A web host is the company that will "rent" you space on the Internet. It's very important that your web host is reliable with very little downtime. Companies like ivoy can be used to host, in addition to registering your domain and other services offered.

These hosts charge a monthly service fee, but have many options for you to use when creating your web site and marketing it. There are free web hosts available, but you will find that their services are limited in terms of marketing tools and bandwidth.

If uploading songs, choose a web host that will give you plenty of bandwidth.

Web hosts can help you register your domain name, offer security for your site, especially if you choose to sell music on it, and can help you with many design details and coding issues.

Many web hosts require you to use their services for at least a year before you will be able to move your domain name to another host. Read all the fine print before signing up.

## FTP CLIENT

In order to upload songs and web content to your site and other places, you will need to be able to communicate with your web host. FTP client programs are the easiest way to do this. The process is simple so don't feel you lack the necessary computer skills. You may not have to worry about finding an FTP client as many of the web site packages offered have this feature built-in. If you do need one, you can search for them online or download Fetch at http://www.fetchsoftworks.com. There are also free tools online such as:

- CuteFTP:

    http://www.cuteftp.com/cuteftp

- CoreFTP:

    http://www.coreftp.com

Don't forget to review your host subscriptions to learn more about what is offered.

# WEB DESIGN

Creating a web design that is easy to navigate should be your first priority. If you know nothing about web design, you can sign up with a host that has templates available for you to choose. These templates will walk you through adding pages, headings, buttons, banners, boxes, and much more.

Keep in mind that when you use templates, your web site may look like someone else's. The trick to distinguishing your site from another musician's is by looking at some of the other web sites online and personalizing yours with band photos, links to your MySpace page, and other items that create a unique feel.

If you want to design a unique site, you will need to learn basic code in order to create pages. There is plenty of software available if you already know HTML, but if you don't, and you don't have the time to learn anything complex, there are web creating software tools that make creating web pages very easy.

Using a technique called "What You See Is What You Get", or WYSIWYG, HTML code is broken down into very simple commands that give you great results. DreamWeaver is one such program. Other Common web site editing tools used by those creating their own web sites include:

- Site Spinner:

    http://www.virtualmechanics.com/products/spinner

- Namo Web Editor:

    http://www.namo.com

These sites include trial versions of their software that you can try.

In order to find a web editor that will give you the finished product you want, research different programs online to see what they can offer. There are also many web site templates that are available for purchase that you can customize. A simple online search will give you lots to choose from, but here're a few to get you started:

- Boxed Art:

http://www.boxedart.com

- Basic Templates:

  http://www.basictemplates.com

If you want to learn more about HTML, one site to check out is http://davesite.com/webstation/html.

Hiring a web designer is also an option.

While you want your site to be eye catching, you don't want to visually impair people with large fonts, bright colors, and extreme graphics. Always think professional and imagine the types of people who will be seeing your site. Your web site should complement your music. You'll Grab attention faster by allowing them to listen to your music easily instead of wasting their time and hiding it behind promotional items, hard to find media players, or in the middle of banner ads.

One of the best items to include on your web site is a site map. This will allow visitors to move around your web site easily. Make sure all important links including your site map are on every page of your web site. A site map could possibly help with search engine SEO as well.

## WEB SITE CONTENT

Web site content is anything you choose to include on your site. Typical content includes:

- Articles

- Pictures (.jpeg, and .gif files are the most common)

- Songs

- Videos

- Ordering pages

- Music and product descriptions

- Blog, Vlogs and Podcasts

- Reviews

- Upcoming events

- Merchandise (t-shirts, mouse pads, etc.)

Many people have trouble deciding how many pages to add to their web site when designing them. It is important not to overwhelm visitors with too much information, overcrowded pages, or pages that are out of sequence.

A rule that will come in handy is to create one page per idea. This means that you should create:

- Home page

- Products page

- Music download page

- About the band page (or pages depending on how much info. you want to put up there

- Upcoming gigs page

- Music reviews page

- Video page

- Ordering page

- Email sign-up page

- Site map

You will also want to include a links page that includes links to other web sites where your work is featured. If you decide to create a podcast you should add a page for that as well. With a web site, you can continually add pages as you go along.

If you need graphics, there are plenty of sites online you can use to find content for your webpage and you can also search the Internet for free graphics to use.

For free button and banner generators some good sites include:

- ButtonGenerator:

  http://www.buttongenerator.com

- Flaming Text:

  http://flamingtext.com/start.html

Web content is what keeps people interested in visiting your site. Updating content often is important. This includes uploading new songs. **VERY** important items to include on your site include:

- EPK (Electronic Promo Kits)

- Band Biography

- Links to social networking sites

# EPK (ELECTRONIC PROMO KITS)

One of the greatest uses for web sites is the option of creating electronic promo kits and making them available to record producers, radio producers, club owners, booking agents, journalists, and others who can be beneficial to your career.

Kits typically include songs, album art, lyrics, video, headshots or concert photos. By placing your URL on your business cards and email, you're able to invite influential people to visit your site and download your EPK.

Create a separate page for EPK's and include a link on your home page so people will be able to find it easily.

You can also send traditional kits to producers and others via snail mail if you chose. The same materials are usually included.

## BAND BIOGRAPHY

Including a well-written, up-to-date band bio is important if you want people to learn more about who you are and the types of music you produce. In order to increase your fan base, you will have to tell them about yourself. This will create an instant connection and prompt new visitors to listen to your songs.

Items to include in the band bio:

- Name of band

- How you chose the name

- Number of years together

- Name of band members

- Instruments and other facts about band members (colleges attended, influences, etc.)

- Favorite song recorded

- Hobbies

- Upcoming gigs

- Include pictures if possible so people get a better idea of who you are.

## LINKS TO SOCIAL NETWORKING SITES

Always include links to social networking sites you may be associated with so fans and others will be able to check them out. Include links on these sites back to your web site as well (called back-links). This will increase your exposure on the web and help search engines find you easily.

The content you choose to put on your web site depends on what you are trying to achieve through the site. If your site is being used to promote your band, then include articles, interviews, songs, and live performances. Update it often to reflect upcoming concerts and other events. If you are using your site to sell CDs and music downloads it might require a slightly different approach.

Think of your web site as your calling card for those who want to know more about the music. Make the content on your site as fun as possible so people will return again and again. Tie in other web sites you are using to market your music. This will not only serve as a way to direct people to your profile pages, but it will also give you the opportunity to create back links to these pages and your web page.

You will learn more about back links and other types of Internet marketing strategies in later sections of this chapter. For now, concentrate on designing a web site that is easy to use and update it often to showcase your music.

## UPLOADING SONGS

You have a few options when it comes to uploading your songs and samples. You can:

- Subscribe to online networks like http://www.snocap.com/ and upload songs so they can be purchased by listeners

- Make songs available for listening right away by streaming them instead of allowing them to be downloaded

- Use a third party media applet to let people download your music from your web site

- Upload songs to podcasting networks and let them be played during podcasts

- If you use any of the aggregators mentioned previously, you can provide a link to iTunes and other sites

The difference between uploading mp3s and streaming your music on your web site is that most mp3 can be downloaded onto the listener's computer. Since downloading songs from the Internet to a computer can take time, streaming your songs is another option. When you stream your songs, visitors can begin listening right away instead of waiting for the download to be complete. Streaming can help you make more sales as the attention span is very short on the Internet.

## CREATING AN MP3

In order to create an mp3, you will need to have ripping and/or converting software on your computer. You can find free versions or you can pay for one on sites including:

- http://www.musicmatch.com

- You can also use iTunes for both Mac and PC

You'll find a full list of software here :

- http://www.hitsquad.com/smm/cat/CD_RIPPERS/

If you want to include mp3s on your web site, I suggest you upload samples that are no longer than 2 minutes long. This will increase interest in your music and, if you are selling your music, it will give listeners enough so they can make up their minds on whether to purchase one or not. Using a third party media applet will allow people to hear your songs easily and prevent them from downloading them. Since most people have Windows Media Player, Real Time Media Player or QuickTime you can also just upload the files, and this makes it easy for people to save your music on their computer.

If you want to add streaming music files on your web site, you will have to add another file called a Metafile. This can be done using your web editor and is necessary if you want to allow visitors to listen to your music without having to download it.

Follow these steps to create streaming music files:

1.  Upload your songs as mp3s and upload them to your web site

2.  Create a text file so your FTP client can find the file easily. (open notepad and type in the file name you chose for the file. Save the file and add m3u at the end of the file name. Ex: www.yoursongs.com/mp3/artist/songtitle.m3u

3.  Upload this new file to the directory that contains your original mp3 file.

4.  Create a link to your web site and test it to be sure the link works

## FLASH AND EMBEDDING MUSIC

If you want to use a flash media player instead of mp3s, you will be protecting your music from Internet theft because it is safer than streaming. Listening to your music is easier for visitors because they won't need to have Windows Media or RealTime Player on their computer.

But some visitors may not be able to view flash, so it is important to mention that you may lose people if they can't hear your music, but this is becoming less and less of a issue.

Wimpy makes some great inexpensive players that are easy to set up on your web site:

- The Wimpy Player:

  http://www.wimpyplayer.com

# UPLOADING VIDEO

Uploading video is similar to uploading music. The idea is to give visitors the opportunity not only to listen to your music, but also see visually how you interpret the music. Video can include anything from live performances, to creating a storyboard and filming action sequences, behind the scenes footage, documentaries, acoustic or unplugged versions of your songs, etc. While this method may be too expensive for most musicians, there are inexpensive options that may allow you to produce high quality videos that will enhance your band's reputation.

These options include:

- Contacting local colleges to see if they have a video production or media major. Most students have to complete projects that include producing video and short films. Contact students to see if they would be willing to shoot a video for their project. In return, you get a high quality video that you can upload to your web site.

- Ask your friends and family if they know anyone who is a video producer or director. They do not have to be famous, just having the knowledge and equipment is enough. You may be able to pay them a small fee or let them use the video in their portfolio.

- Take a class on shooting film or video. There are many small technical colleges and universities that offer these classes each semester. If you have to complete a project, you will be able to use the school's equipment or get great deals on equipment.

- You can create a decent video using a small digital camera. Shop around online or borrow someone else's. Shoot your video and then use a free editing program like Windows Movie Maker or Apple iMovie.

- Instead of using live video, shoot a series of artwork or still shots and string them together using the software mentioned above. This a great way to create something new and interesting.

Uploading your video can be carried out in a very similar way to uploading your music. You can also just put a YouTube link on your webpage and have the YouTube player embedded on your site. That also creates some great back-links.

Video can add a new dimension to your web site and make it more interactive. Upload your video on social networking sites like MySpace, YouTube, and Facebook for even more exposure.

# GENERATING ONLINE BUZZ

By this point, you should have a good understanding of creating a web site, adding content, and uploading songs and video. After doing all this, you may notice you are not getting the response you thought you would. If you haven't begun marketing your web site, you need to start at this point as this is the only way you will be able to attract visitors.

Some of the best ways to market your site include:

- Tell everyone you know you have a web site

- Join forms and online music groups

- Start an email list

- If selling your music, find an online distributor or use IODA or Tunecore as mentioned before. These aggregators put you on many online portals such as iTunes, Rhapsody, etc. and you only need to send it to them once!

- Sign up on music search engines

- Exchange links with other musicians

- Use SEO

- Banner ads and other Internet marketing

- Use offline methods (t-shirts, business cards, fliers, etc.)

- Offering free stuff

Marketing is very time consuming, but once you have attracted a few people to your site, it will become easier. This is where word-of-mouth advertising begins. Imagine every person who visits your web site tells another person about it. The number of people you can reach is immeasurable. Online marketing has changed the way word-of-mouth advertising begins, making it easier to get the ball rolling.

In later chapters, you will learn how to use the Internet to your advantage and how to market your music through podcasts, blogs, and other methods.

## WHAT IS SEO?

A common term you may have heard or read about while conducting your research is SEO, or Search Engine Optimization. This is how search engines find your web site, MySpace profile, or any other information you have posted online and includes it in a user's search. SEO can be used to increase web rankings for those online when they include the right keywords (search terms used to find topics online) on their pages.

You can use keywords in your web site, profile page, and in your Squidoo pages that will help you obtain a higher web ranking on search results pages.

Most people only look at the top five search engine results when they are browsing web sites. If you can get into the top five or ten, your web site will be viewed more often.

You can register your web site with search engines. This is very easy and free. Visit various search engines and fill out a simple form. This will let search engines know that you exist, but it is by no means the only way to attract a search engine's attention. In fact in many cases it's better to let the search engines find you rather than submitting it to them.

The best search engines to market your web site on include:

- Google

- Yahoo

- MSN

These sites are widely used and increase your chances of being found.

In addition to registering your entire web site, you can also register individual pages. This is a good option if you plan on selling your CD or digital music. Register description pages and any other pages you think would be of interest.

The best way to use keywords is by integrating them into your web content. Using one keyword four or five times should be enough to be noticed by web spiders (automatic programs that are looking for keywords entered by those searching on the Internet). To find popular keywords use free tools found on Google or Yahoo or simple think of what you would type in if you were searching.

One of the most effective places to put keywords is in the titles of your web pages. When search engines are looking for relevant pages to include in search lists, they use "web spiders," which capture information and bring it back. Web spiders don't want to do too much work, so they will check title pages first in order to find the keywords they are looking for. Capture the spider's attention and you will be included on the list.

Another great way to attract web spiders is by using back-links. These are links that direct people to and from areas on the Internet you are advertising on. This may be your MySpace page, personal blog, or other social networking site. Back-links can also be added to articles you publish online. Add back-links whenever you can and make sure you add them to you web site.

Links within your web site are effective for several reasons. Not only will they help visitors navigate through your site, they can help attract attention from web spiders. Use them to direct people to your product pages, ordering pages, or music download pages. Much like graphics and other visual aids, don't overuse links on your pages. One or two is enough for each page. Add a menu bar that appears at the top of each page if you want visitors to be able to find certain pages quickly.

Be aware that adding too many keywords in your web content will get your site flagged as spam, so do your best to incorporate these words into your content as neatly and organically as possible. Don't make a list of the keywords on your web site either, as this is not considered good practice and your web site may be removed if this is discovered. Place keywords in the title and the articles on your page in order to attract more attention from web spiders.

When creating your web site, put keywords into the "meta tags" section of your HTML code. This is very easy to find within your text editor and you can ask your web hosting company for help. Also add the letter "s" to each word you use as an alternative and use misspelled words as well. Many people searching on the Internet may not know the correct spelling of "guitar," for example!

While this was once the weapon of choice by most marketers, there are many other ways to increase your ranking.

Keep in mind that the best way to be noticed on the Internet by search engines is through your popularity. You can influence your online popularity by advertising using pay-per-click ads, which can be inexpensive if done correctly, and a great way to drive traffic to your site.

Pay-per-click ads are effective if they are placed in the right areas on the Internet. Each time a person clicks on your ad, you will have to pay a certain amount, usually determined in an auction style based on demand and the quality of your ad's relevance to the keyword used to search. You can put a ceiling on the most you are willing to pay, and many times you will pay less than that. In addition, as your ad's relevancy goes higher they will charge you less than a competitor of less relevancy.

It could be tricky however to use pay-per-click for a music band unless you have something unique to offer or there is a demand for your merchandise. Use pay-per-click advertising after you have found markets that are interested in your web site. Wait a few months to see if you will need to use this type of marketing. By making use of social networking sites, podcasts, and playing live, you may not need to pay for advertising.

You can increase your popularity in other ways as well by submitting press releases, articles, writing a blog, and using social networking sites. Don't worry too much about being number one on search engine lists, this takes too much effort. There are plenty of other marketing tools to use online that will yield similar results.

## OFFERING FREE STUFF

In the next section, you will learn more about selling your music online, but in the meantime, you should consider how to entice people to go from browsing your web site to making a purchase. The answer is free stuff. Allowing people to preview your music, get an unreleased song for free, enter contests to win CDs or merchandise, or receive discounts on merchandise you are selling are all great ways to generate interest.

Free stuff can also come in the form of:

- Free pictures

- Free shipping

- Free t-shirts or any other merchandise with music purchase

- Coupons

- Special sales on CDs or music downloads
- Free downloads

You'd be surprised what the term "free shipping" can do for your business!

One final rule to follow is to only offer a few freebies at a time. Too many and your customer will become overwhelmed and leave your site. Make the offers special by only offering them for a certain amount of time and encourage customers to act now, before it is no longer available. Most people are motivated more by fear of losing something they want than of gaining it.

## ONLINE CONTESTS

An online contest can be a great way to promote your music and help build your email list. Offering your CD or music download in a drawing or offering other merchandise you may have on your web site once or twice a year encourages visitors to leave their email addresses.

If visitors don't win your music, they are more likely to buy it anyway. This is a good marketing tool that does not cost too much and is another way for you to interact with fans.

## SELLING MUSIC ONLINE

While the idea of selling your music online is an exciting adventure, you need to be prepared. Selling anything online requires you to have a sound business plan and marketing strategy in order for your venture to be successful.

Common questions you should ask yourself:

- Who will handle shipping?
- Who will handle packaging?
- Who will handle making copies of my CD?
- Do I want to sell my music or CD on a music web site or through my own web site?
- How will payments be made?
- Should I incorporate my business?
- How much can I invest in this venture?
- What types of marketing do I have in place?
- What types of policies will I have for returning items?
- Do I want to allow people from other countries to purchase my music or CD?

You have options when it comes to producing and distributing your music online, which is why I encourage people to do so once they have answered the tough questions.

Be realistic. You might not be have the time or the desire to handle all the tasks required to successfully market and distribute your CD unless you make it a full-time job. Why? Because marketing itself will take a large chunk of your time. Secondly, you will have to fill orders yourself, which means boxing and shipping them to the correct addresses if a physical CD. While this task may not seem like much, try shipping five hundred CDs per week.

In addition to administrative paperwork (withholding money for taxes, supplies, additional copies, and storage space, etc.), you may want to have some time to devote to new songs. This is a lot of work even for the most disciplined of people.

There is help, however, but you will have to sacrifice some of the profits in order to sell more CDs. While this may seem like a gamble, if your CD is successful, the money will be well spent.

## CREATING AN ONLINE MUSIC STORE

While selling and distributing your music will require some of your time, there is software and companies that can handle many of the details for you.

One of the best places to sell your music online is CDBaby. For a small fee (around $35.00 per CD title), you can open an account, and CDBaby will create a sales page with ordering details. They will also place samples of your music for visitors to listen to. CDBaby will take care of payment, shipping, and allow you to link your web site directly to their shopping cart program so you will be able to accept credit cards, debit cards, paypal, and other payments. They will also restock your CD when supplies run low.

CDBaby also has a toll-free number that people can call if they don't want to place an order online. This type of customer service will help you sell even more CDs.

For each CD you sell, CDBaby will take a commission of $4.00. The rest is your profit. Each month, you will receive payment from the company for each CD you sell.

If you want to use another company's shopping cart with credit card payment options, but you don't want to have them ship your CD to customers, another site you should take a look at is CCNow at http://www.ccnow.com. The advantage of CCNow is that they will take less commission on the sale of your CD because you will be handling all shipping and restocking issues.

CCNow has a monthly fee of $9.95. You will have to pay this fee even if you don't sell anything for the month, but if you are consistently selling CD's, then you will make more money than using CDBaby.

Limitations to CCNow include restrictions on selling digital downloads, which is a must as downloads are quickly becoming the preferred choice of many. But as you will read later, there are other places to sell downloads.

Opening a merchant account and setting up your own shopping cart using computer software is a third option to consider especially if you are making more than three hundred a month in CD sales on CDBaby or CCNow.

Merchant accounts are easy to open and are used to help you process credit card orders. You will have to go through a standard credit check in order to be approved, and you will have to pay a monthly fee that could be as much as $75.00. But if sales are good, this is less than what you would be paying if you stayed with the other merchant sites.

Once you have your merchant account, you will have to find shopping cart programs online that can be used to process orders. Most have a monthly fee, so make sure you budget for this expense.

If you decide to run your online music store using a merchant account, keep in mind that you will still be responsible for shipping and stocking your CD. You will be able to sell digital downloads if you decide to use this option, however.

You should allow as many payment options as possible as some people do not trust sites like or don't have Paypal accounts. Limiting your customers will also limit the amount of money you can make on your sales. If you don't have the time to ship CDs or handle web site maintenance, you should choose a company like CDBaby to help you with these details.

## DIGITAL DOWNLOADS

Digital downloads are becoming more popular since they can be purchased on the computer or through some cell phone devices instantly. People who want to create digital music collections by downloading their favorite songs or entire albums are doing so through sites like iTunes and Rhapsody.

To take advantage of this new trend, you have a few options. As mentioned above, you can sell digital downloads through your web site when you open a merchant account.

If using CDBaby, you can sign up for their digital distribution option. Your songs will be posted on the sites mentioned above and many others. CDBaby takes a small commission fee (9%) for each CD they sell digitally and you keep the rest.

In order to make the most money and gain more exposure online, I suggest you take advantage of selling your CD in both digital and standard formats. Consider particularly selling single songs as downloads as well. And keep the 2 previous aggregators we mentioned earlier in mind, to get your music into all the important digital online stores. Here they are again:

- http://www.iodalliance.com/

- http://www.tunecore.com/

A healthy email list can be one of your best tools when marketing your music. Later in this book we'll get into more details regarding strategies on building a mailing list.

## WEB SITE MAINTENANCE

Making sure your web site is functional at all times is one of the most important ways to keep people coming to your site. If a visitor tries to view your web site and is unsuccessful, the chances of them trying again are greatly decreased.

Consistently check to make sure that all the links are functioning properly. Also make sure all of your web pages are still listed with search engines. As your web site grows, make sure to add new pages to these search engines.

## BENEFITS OF SELLING MUSIC AND BUILDING A WEB SITE

I know that selling your music online may seem overwhelming at first, but once you decide what you want to handle and what you don't, you will find the process is much easier and a lot of fun. Receiving monthly or weekly checks from these sites will make selling your music worth it.

Building a web site regardless of whether you want to sell CDs yourself is worth it because a professional web site will attract a lot of attention, especially when competing with other musicians on sites like MySpace who don't have personal web sites of their own.

Marketing your web site will be an ongoing process you should use in conjunction with social networking sites. Adding back-links to your web site and networking sites can give people more opportunities to find you when searching for your music. It will also help your web ranking.

While you should be concerned with your web ranking, it should not become your mission to be #1. Most web sites do not stay at #1 for too long, and you have plenty of other tasks to complete when marketing your music. Keep in mind the SEO is important, but it is just another way of marketing your music.

# Chapter 8
▸ **Article Marketing Strategies**

Once you have designed your web site you will have to begin marketing it online. This can be done in a number of ways, but if you want to see results fast, writing articles and publishing them online is one of the most powerful ways to market your music.

There are literally thousands of online publications and newsletters for you to submit articles to. If you are targeting a specific group of music lovers, conduct a search to find publications that are of interest to this group. Contact the web master or online publisher and ask them to consider your article. Many sites even have contributing author pages where you can submit articles or inquire about submission criteria.

Conduct Google searches to find some of the most popular ezines.

## WRITING ARTICLES

You are probably asking yourself what you should write about. The best advice is to write about what you know and what you are passionate about when it comes to music. The most important aspect to article writing is to give readers information they can use or find worthy of reading again or passing on to others. If you teach music on the side, write some informational articles about teaching music, tips on becoming a music teacher or tips on playing a particular instrument. You can write about the process of recording your music or putting together a tour. Write about the good or bad experiences you had when booking your shows. Tell others what they should look out for.

You can also write music reviews, current trends in the music scene, or pieces about performers you enjoy. Use your imagination and write articles that mean something to you.

If you feel you can't write, consider paying a writer to write for you. Try http://www.exquisitewriting.com for assistance or one of the online freelance sites. They can get you started and after going through a few you should be able to get a feel for it and start writing on your own in a short time.

One of the most important items to include in your article submission is your signature name and link to your web site address. This will give people the means to find out more about you if they choose. Even if you are publishing articles on your own web site, add your address. A good way to increase your marketing potential is to allow others to publish articles you have on your web site on their sites as well. This is why including your web address is so important.

## HOW ARE ARTICLES USED?

This is a good question as once you allow your article to by published, chances are it will be reprinted. One of the easiest ways to gain more exposure and cover more ground on the Internet is by having an article included in a newsletter. This will give you access to all the members of the email list without you having to do any work.

Those who read the newsletter are more likely to check out your web site and profile pages because your article is included. Try to get your articles printed in as many places as possible.

## WRITING AN EFFECTIVE BYLINE

When writing articles, the content you provide is not how you will be drawing people to your site. It is your byline that will direct people. While the article itself should be well written and contain valuable information, your byline should also contain contact information and a short introduction to your music.

A typical byline for a musician should look like this:

> Johnny Music is the lead vocalist for The B Sharps. Their new release, "NightSessions." and concert events can be found at www.mybandxxxx.com. Johnny is also a guitar teacher, singer and songwriter.

Even though this byline is only three lines, it provides relevant background information, a plug for new music, and the URL to the web site, enough to drive people to the site.

## GETTING YOUR ARTICLES PUBLISHED

Three ways to get your music articles published are:

- Look for Ezines that accept submissions

- Query music Ezines and ask if they are interested in your article

- Submit articles to article databases

All ezines need content, which means that many have submission guidelines and deadlines for submissions. If you have a favorite ezine or you know of one that is popular, find out their guidelines and submit your article.

It is very important that you adhere to word count, font size, and file type when submitting an article. If you don't follow the ezine's guidelines, your article may be rejected without even being read.

Some ezines want to know what your article is about before they will accept it. Sending a well-written query letter outlining your article will increase your chances of seeing it published.

Query letters are not difficult to write. Start your letter with a simple introduction and include why you are an expert on the topic of your article. Then add the first paragraph of your article as a way to entice editors. Conclude your letter with contact information and a greeting.

It may take a few weeks to get a reply so don't worry if you don't hear back immediately. Don't submit the same article anywhere else until you have heard back from the editors of the first place to which you've submitted it.

Unless the publication specifically says they accept reprints, try not submit the article anywhere else. Some writers will submit their articles while waiting on a reply because they want to have it published quickly. If you do this and the article is accepted somewhere else that restricts reprints, you should let the other ezine know that the article has been accepted elsewhere.

Many times, those in need of content will share their opt-in email list with you. This means you will be able to reach more people by sending them your newsletter, event updates, and other information.

If you want your article to appear in many online publications at one time, the best way to accomplish this is by submitting it to an online article database such as:

- EzineArticles.com: http://www.ezinearticles.com

- Ideamarketers.com: http://www.ideamarketers.com

EzineArticles is one of the more important ones. The reason the articles they have are listed and ranked high on Google is the combination of wisely used keywords and the fact that Google has chosen EzineArticles over other competing sites.

While you won't be paid for your article, your web site will appear in the byline beside your name so people will be able to visit your site. Many ezines, newsletters, web sites, and education sites use these articles to educate or entertain visitors. Articles are free and anyone can use them as long as they give writers credit for them.

Later, you will learn more about Squidoo, which is an information site that is also used to increase web ranking and overall exposure. Publishing articles on sites like Squidoo can really help people find you.

# USING ARTICLES FOR YOUR WEB SITE

If you are looking for additional content for your site, you can download free articles from the web sites mentioned above. This is a great way to save time on writing all the articles yourself and you will probably be helping out other musicians as well.

# OTHER WAYS TO REACH PEOPLE ONLINE

In addition to writing articles, you can also:

- Write press releases

- Write concert reviews for online publications

- Write music reviews

- Create your own newsletter

- Submit your music for review

Writing articles and creating other documents can help you reach groups that may not use social networking sites. By adding your web address, you will also increase your web ranking.

Consider writing a few articles to post on your web site at the minimum if you choose not to send them elsewhere. If you can give valuable informative information or insights on music related topics, it will prompt people to take a closer look at what you have to offer.

A newsletter is an extension of your web site and can be used in a variety of different ways. You can use a newsletter to:

- Inform fans of upcoming events

- Promote your new CD or music

- Inform fans and others of new links, feeds, or podcasts that are on your web site

- Offer freebies and discounts to increase sales

- Educate and entertain your fans

Newsletters can be sent monthly, quarterly, or twice a year. It will depend on what you want to include in the newsletter and how much time you have to prepare it. If you are allowed to use the email list of ezines you submit articles to, consider publishing a monthly newsletter in order to attract more attention quickly.

Submitting your music so it can be reviewed by an ezine is another way to increase your exposure. While you should be hopeful for a good review, any review will help you. In the article, your band name, web site, song titles, album titles, and other information about your music will be mentioned.

Have someone review your music when you are about to release a new CD or when you will be playing live.

Chapter 9
# ▸ Squidoo

Earlier in this book, I mentioned a web site called Squidoo. On this site, you will find thousands of articles on various topics.

While the site was created to share information on the Internet, many affiliate marketers and others have found that Squidoo can also be used to increase their exposure on popular search engines like Google. Using Squidoo is easy and can help you with the following:

- Increase your web presence

- Create an email list

- Quick indexing on Google, sometimes as fast as 2-3 days!

- High Google rankings

By creating one or two page "lenses" using popular keywords, you will be able to increase visitors to your web site and increase your sales.

## USING SQUIDOO TO PROMOTE EZINE ARTICLES

Writing articles about your band, music in general, or the music industry is one tool you can use to promote your music online. But how do you showcase your articles after submitting them to article directories like EzineArticles.com?

Using a Squidoo lens is a powerful strategy to do this. With so many articles uploaded into the EzineArticles directory, you will have to find ways to stand out. Creating a lens and using it to help search engines find your article is an easy way to accomplish this task. And, since Google loves Squidoo, it will be picked up more often by Google's web spiders.

The higher ranking your articles receive, the more they will be viewed. In order to use Squidoo effectively, you will have to find keywords that are the most popular and then create lenses around these keywords. It is a very simple process once you identify these keywords.

# FINDING THE RIGHT KEYWORDS

Before you write any lenses on Squidoo, you should determine the keywords that are the most popular and related to your subject. Each lens you create should be centered on a different keyword. You can create lenses for your articles, press releases, web site, your MySpace profile page or other social networking sites. But without the right keywords, your lens isn't going to be that successful.

# GOOGLE ADWORDS

If you are unsure as to which keywords you should use, you can visit Google or Yahoo! and use their keyword search tools. It won't cost you anything but it is a helpful tool for choosing the right keywords. There are also software programs that you can purchase, that will provide a more in-depth list of keywords than you would get from free tools.

Here are the Google and Yahoo direct links:

- https://adwords.google.com/select/KeywordToolExternal

- http://inventory.overture.com/d/searchinventory/suggestion

When beginning your search, choose a niche, or target group, that you want to market to. The genre of music you play, a specific instrument, or artists that are similar to yours are all niches that would work. After entering in a niche keyword or a keyword phrase, a list will pop up that will give you the top keywords used to find more information about these niches. These are actual keywords used by those searching for information online.

If your niche is too general, you may need to narrow your choices. For example, if your music genre is "rock," narrow your niche to "classic rock" or "contemporary rock." It's also interesting to note that 3 and 4 word key phrases at the moment seem easier in regards to getting a high rank on Google, but by no means is this a definitive rule.

Choose the top three or four keywords. These are the words that you will use to create your Squidoo lens.

# GOOGLE SEARCHES

Another way to find keywords is to conduct searches of your own to see which web sites pop up when you plug in certain keywords. While this method may take a little longer, you may be able to create a unique list that your web site or profile pages fit into.

Keywords will change from time to time, so each time you create a lens on Squidoo, you should research keywords so you can use the most popular.

Here's a highly effective strategy for finding keywords. This is so powerful that you'll be amazed how fast you can rank high. Type in the keyword that best describes your article into the search box on the EzineArticles web site. This will give you EzineArticles' top ranked articles on Google. If you type in the same keyword into the Google search engine, chances are those same EzineArticles will appear on the first page. If you find the same articles listed, then create a Squidoo lens around this keyword.

Since you will be uploading your articles to EzineArticles, creating a Squidoo lens to go along with it is a win-win situation that does not take too much time and has outstanding results. Squidoo out performs EzineArticles on Google.

You can also use EzineArticles to look up subcategories for even more keywords. Subcategories are used to promote specific topics or to narrow down a general category. Most topics can be whittled down into subcategories. Decide which subcategories your article can be included in and check out the articles listed. Note which keywords are in their titles as this will give you a good idea of which to use when creating lenses.

Here is how to employ this strategy. Go to EzineArticles.com's home page and click on a category in the middle of the page, for example "Arts and Entertainment." Then choose "Music" from the subcategories that appear. These articles are not necessarily the top ranked in Google. From these articles click and open the first one. At the bottom of this articles page will be a "Most Viewed EzineArticles in the 'Arts and Entertainment: Music Category.'" This will call up the top 15 articles.

These articles are probably at the top because Google has ranked them on the first page. Choose one related to your topic. Are there some common keywords in these top articles? Look at the titles and this will give you the important keywords. These articles should contain keywords that are similar to each other and will give you a good idea about which keywords people who are searching the Internet are using.

Keep in mind that those who wrote the most popular articles are doing their research when choosing keywords. Follow their lead and save yourself some time by using their keywords.

## CREATING A SQUIDOO LENS

Online article sites like EzineArticles do not want people to sell items through their articles, and this limits what you can include in the article.

Fortunately, you can include your web site in your byline and signature.

This is why many online businesses use Squidoo. In addition to giving their articles more exposure online, businesses can create lenses that promote what they have to sell. While lenses should be informative, you can include information about your web site, specifics about your CD or music, and ways that people can order it.

Creating a Squidoo lens is simple and is a way for you to write about your band or latest CD. You can easily register and be able to start building your lens within minutes. Those who use Squidoo often are able to create four or five lenses within an hour! Once you know what to put in the lens, the rest becomes much easier.

## DEFINING YOUR NICHE

While the lenses you will create will have a music theme, it is important to develop a niche within the music category so you can become recognized as an expert. Those who are perceived as experts will have their lenses viewed more times than those who are not.

Possible niches for your needs include:

- Types of music you play
- Aspects of the music industry
- How you write songs
- Working with other musicians
- Selling CDs and music downloads
- Music reviews
- Sound systems and equipment
- Live performance tips
- Studio and recording tips

You can choose more than one niche, but try to center your lens around one niche at a time. This will help you build a stable of lenses that will be viewed by many people.

If you need additional ideas for topics, go to:

- http://www.squidoo.com/browse/top_lenses/traffic

You will find a listing of the top 100 lenses. While most of them will not be music related, you will be able to see what people are searching for when they are on the Squidoo site.

## CREATING A LENS

It's easy to sign up for membership on Squidoo. At the upper right of the home page http://www.squidoo.com/ a link is provided for you to sign up. Just enter your name, e-mail, username, and password. You're ready to create your first lens.

Click on the "Create a Lens" button. Your first step is inputting the subject of your lens in the "My lens is about" field. This is not the title of your lens but should include your keyword phrase. Go to step 2.

Select "I just want to do my own thing." This will provide you with a default layout for your lens that is easily adjusted. Go to step 3.

Here you will need to choose the title of your lens. Make sure to include the keyword phrase!

Choosing a URL for your lens is the next step. Try to match your keyword phrase separated by a dash. An example would be:

> http://www.squidoo.com/funk-guitar

If this name is already taken, then put "-1" after the last word:

> http://www.squidoo.com/funk-guitar-1

Search engines will not be affected by numbers, so don't be concerned about them.

Using your keywords in the URL is important, as Google will give you a higher ranking. The dash in between your keywords will also help as Google sees each keyword as a separate keyword, but it is not crucial.

Next, pick your category and the rating for your lens (safe for all ages, etc). Go on to step 4.

Here you will add your top keyword or keyword phrase, which should also be in your title. Then add an additional 3 of your top keywords for your niche under the "And 3 more good ones are" section. You can use the other high-ranking keywords you found during your search. You'll be able to add more keywords or "Tags" later but NEVER go over 20 tags as your lens might get deleted.

Since Squidoo will advertise affiliate links on your lens that coincide with your lens topic, you will be paid a percentage for each sale that is made through the link! Currently they pay out 50%. While it might not add up to much it can give you a little extra money each month. You will need to choose your payment options on the right under the section where you can edit your tags.

## DESIGNING YOUR LENS

This part is pretty easy and should not take too long to complete. The first item to add to your lens is a short bio about yourself and a picture. This will let people know that you are serious about what you have to say and that you are an "expert." Your bio should include your web address or MySpace URL. This is how you create back-links. Tell people a little about your music and your career. Don't click on the option "Make this your default bio" as you should have a custom bio specific for each of your lenses.

After writing your bio, you will be able to starting creating the content for the lens.

Your lens' Introduction is what will be read by most people. This section should include relevant information about what your lens is about. If you are writing about Hip Hop, for example, you may want to focus on artists that have influenced you over the years, who you think is the best in the genre, or how Hip Hop has changed over the years.

In order to keep your lens from being deleted because it was mistaken as spam, it is best to have at least 4 "Modules" on each of your lenses. Squidoo modules are just interactive content boxes for you to add as you see fit. These include Amazon, ebay, Guestbook, Write, etc.

In the Write module you can upload two or three other free articles that were not written by you from the previous mentioned web sites such as EzineArticles. Also if there are reviews of your work, a free article you found online about Hip Hop, or the online store URL where you are selling your music you can make a second write module and add it there. Adding a back-link to the source is a good idea as well.

If adding articles written by others, make sure you have permission to use them first and always include the author's name so they receive proper credit.

Add an image or two as well. This could include a Hip Hop artist you have written about, your CD cover, or other image that pertains to your lens.

You should include your keyword in the articles you place on your lens that you have written. Keywords should be used 4 or 5 times in order to be picked up by search engines.

After creating your lens, you are ready to upload it. You can write other lenses on various music related topics if you choose. Just make sure you always include valuable information that people will want to read.

Spammers are not allowed on Squidoo and your lenses will be erased if you try to sell your product too much.

Let the keywords do the work for you. Mentioning your web site is fine, but don't overdo it.

## FILLING YOUR LENS WITH CONTENT

Most lenses are merely a page long. This includes written content, contact information, and other web sites that offer additional information.

If you are writing a niche article about a music industry topic, make sure it is filled with valuable information and that it is brief. One or two paragraphs should be enough. While it is important for you to be brief, you want to include all relevant information so people will want to visit your web site or read your article. Browse through other lenses to see what is included and what is not.

Since most people browse through lenses quickly when looking for information, the introduction is where you should devote the most energy. After writing your main content, make sure to include your web site information.

## MAINTAINING YOUR LENS

The great thing about Squidoo is that you can add new content easily but you do not need to do it as often as a blog. Creating 10 or 12 lenses should be enough to increase your presence and drive traffic to your site.

## BENEFITS OF SQUIDOO

As you can see, the benefits of creating lenses on Squidoo are many. Since this web site is relatively new, its impact on search engines like Google has been very strong.

Using Squidoo, you have an endless amount of topics and keywords to choose from. If you upload articles and press releases, you can use Squidoo to highlight them as well.

Another great benefit is the time it takes to create a lens. Once your lens is complete, you can leave it alone. The maintenance is low when compared to uploading new content to your web site, blog or MySpace page.

You will find codes you can use that will enhance your Squidoo lens and make it stand out to people who will want to view it in the bonus chapters at the end of this book.

Other ways to increase the power of your lens include:

- Joining Squidoo groups. Groups are lists of different Squidoo lenses that are related to one another. Click on the "Groups" link on the top, in the middle of the Squidoo site to join a group. In the middle of that page, on top again, you can click "Group" one more time to click the sub menus "explore" to get a list of different group categories and "top 100 groups" to see the 100 most popular groups. Join every group that is related to your lens subject.

- Creating an RSS feed. Squidoo lenses have option modules for you to use when you want to update fans and others about the latest news about your band. More about RSS feeds later in this book.

- Creating a mailing list. Squidoo is a great forum for this type of marketing. You'll find more on this later as well.

- Changing the introduction to your lenses every couple of months so people will have new content to view.

Squidoo lenses make it easier for those who have a limited amount of time to market their web site, MySpace profile page, and other pages online. If you want to instantly see your web ranking go up, then I strongly recommend creating a few lenses highlighting specific areas of your web site, blog and profile pages.

Chapter 10
# ▶ Social Bookmarking, Back-links and Pinging

In this chapter we will use Squidoo lenses as the example. These strategies work exceptionally well for Squidoo, however they work just as well for your blogs and web site. So where we talk about Squidoo lenses you can easily substitute your blog or web site.

What are back-links? Back-links are incoming links to a web site or web page from another web page or web site. The number of back-links is an indication of the popularity or importance of that web site or page and is a factor in determining your page rank (PR rank) and placement on search engines.

Adding back-links to your Squidoo lenses will help increase your ranking. You can use sites like Onlywire, Digg and http://del.icio.us/ to create high PR back-links quickly. In this chapter we will focus on Onlywire and Digg.

If you are not getting indexed fast enough or your lens or web site is not holding steady, it is probably because you do not have enough quality back-links.

## ONLYWIRE

First sign up at http://onlywire.com/

The next step will take you to a page to input your login info for all the sites they include. You'll have to go to each site you want to use and sign up if you do not have a account already. For ease of use, I would use the same login info for each site. When finished, click "Create My Account."

Then click and drag the "Save Page (std)" to your toolbar where you have your bookmarks or favorites. This is really very simple and if you click "need Help" it will show you exactly how to do this. Only use "Save Page (std)," do not use "Save Page (fr)." This uses frames and can be problematic.

Now go to your lens page on Squidoo. After it finishes loading hit the "Save Page (std)" bookmark in your toolbar that you just made.

On this page add different tags that relate to your Squidoo lens subject. Add your tags separating each word with a space. If the tags are more than one word put a dash in between each word. For example:

- Hip-hop-rappers rap-music rappers hip-hop-music-beats

Add related tags until the field is full.

Next write a short description of your lens making sure to use your main keyword in the description! Then click "Bookmark Page" and your lens is submitted to every social bookmarking site on onlywire, currently 19 sites. If this seems confusing you'll find it's very intuitive when you actually do it, so don't worry. This is a proven strategy to generate some great high PR back-links!

Do not submit too many lenses on the same topic too quickly or the social bookmarking sites that Onlywire submits to on your behalf might look at you as a spammer and delete your account. Spacing out your submissions is the best policy.

# DIGG

Digg.com is another useful tool:

- http://digg.com/

Here is how you can "Digg" your Squidoo lens or other articles.

Go to your Squidoo lens URL such as:

- http://squidoo.com/myband/

Click on the "digg" button. Usually this is found on the right side of the page though it is sometimes found on the left.

In the "Story Title" field use your lens keywords as before.

Under "Story Description" give a brief review of what your lens is about using some of your keywords.

For the topic, just click the subject relating to your lens.

That's it. You're done!

Please note. Digg is very aggressive and will not hesitate to delete your account if they consider you a spammer. You must be very cautious and not submit the same lens topics from one account too often. It is good to have multiple dig accounts to give you more flexability.

This will help boost your page ranks and can send many more visitors to your web site.

## THE IMPORTANCE OF PINGING

Another way to increase your exposure online is to register lenses and blogs with a ping service. A ping service will broadcast your lens to those sites that publish web content. Creating back-links on various sites on the Internet is the goal when using a ping site.

Two of the best are:

- http://pingomatic.com/
- http://pingoat.com/

It is very easy to register your lens or blog. Let's go thru the steps involved with Pingomatic.

Place your lens title into the first box under "Blog Name."

Add the lens URL underneath "Blog Home Page."

Add the lens RSS URL underneath "RSS URL" if you are using a RSS Feed. This is optional.

Select the services to ping and the special services by clicking next to each relevant box.

The last step is to click "Send Pings." Your lens will be sent to different directories on the Internet.

As mentioned before, do not abuse this. Make sure to space them out so you won't be considered a spammer.

## Chapter 11
▶ **Email Lists and Autoresponders**

Building a list is an important part of any marketing campaign. Many people believe it is difficult to do, that it takes too much time or that it is very complicated. This is simply not true. There are many ways to have much of the work automatically done for you as well as various sources to get the forms generated for you to put on your webpage, blog or Squidoo Lens.

It is absolutely vital that you find a way to communicate with your visitors after they have left your site. Email lists and autoresponders are a way you can achieve this. Sending out emails is an easy way to get your message across and spark interest.

Email lists can be used in a variety of ways, including:

- Promoting your new music

- Advertising your podcast, webcast, or latest video

- Informing people about upcoming events

- Sharing your newsletter

- Encouraging others to tell their friends about your music

- Connect on a personal level with fans

Email lists are used to start viral marketing campaigns, increase web rankings and encourage those who haven't been to your site in a while to visit.

Include an email form on your site where people can sign up. Keep in mind that you'll need some kind of an offer that entices people to sign up.

Offers include:

- Free pictures

- Newsletters

- Free downloads

- Contests

- Un-Released Music

- Membership to your fan club

## CREATING A MAILING LIST

If you want to create a mailing list so you can email fans about upcoming gigs, CDs, and other events, one of the best ways to get people to sign up for your mailing list is by giving away something for free. People love free stuff! And many are willing to give you their email addresses in order to get it.

Free stuff can be anything from free downloads to free ebooks. You can write a short ebook on how to prepare for a live performance, for example.

Another idea is to compile a bunch of free articles that can be pulled from sites like EzineArticles.

You will be able to reuse materials as long as you aren't making a profit by selling them and you give the proper credit. Always provide the source and author.

Check with your web host to create an email sign up page that allows people to sign up and download your free ebook.

You will need a code to generate your web form in order to start gathering names and emails. Once you have this code you can paste it into your web site, blog or Squidoo lens. Later in this chapter you will learn more about how to get this code.

As you build your email list, you will be able to start viral marketing campaigns that can help boost name recognition. Use this list to alert your fans to worthy events.

Find ways to make signing up for your email lists fun for visitors. Humor is always a powerful quality. Continue to build your email list as you go along and you'll be surprised how fast it builds.

In your email, you should include your band name, web address, and logo so people can easily click and go to your web site or MySpace page.

Make sure to advertise your free ebook and other items on your MySpace page, web site, and when performing live.

## AUTORESPONDERS

Autoresponders are "email on demand" bots that make your information available 24 hours a day, 365 days per year and can dramatically increase your results. Once you write an email you do not need to worry about it until you decide to update it or stop it. You can even write a series of email letters and schedule them. For example, you can send the first letter immediately on sign up and the next letter 2 days after that and then the 3rd letter 2 days after that. This is all done automatically for you.

The most important feature of auto responders however is that they capture the email addresses of people who have requested information allowing you to follow up with them. They will also feature the ability to "unsubscribe" or "opt out" of your email list for those that no longer are interested. Usually this is as simple as the person clicking a link in your email. This is vital in order to not only be respectful but to comply with unsolicited email or "spam" laws.

Autoresponders will gather the names and emails of people who have signed up and give you all sorts of ways to arrange them. They have the ability to give you valuable information such as the exact time they signed up, the state or even the country where they are located. They can even tell you what link was clicked on in your email or email form.

Another great feature of some autoresponder services is that they will generate the code for you to paste into your web site for the web form. Aweber is one autoresponder service that does this. A web form does not necessarily need to be on the page, it can be a pop up, pop under, slide in and many other variations. You can pick the colors to make these forms match your web site, Squidoo page or other site. This is easy to do and if you check with your autoresponder service they will tell you exactly how to do this. You will need to copy and paste the HTML code they provide onto your webpage and then upload your page to your server.

Here is another great feature. The emails that the autoresponder sends out can automatically insert any field you've collected in your form. For example, if you collect first names and email addresses and have a thousand people on your list, you can send all 1000 customized to include the person's first name.

In your form you can also include fields like birthday. Keep the form limited to only the most necessary information, as people are less inclined to sign up if they need to type in too much information. Web attention span is short.

An autoresponder is aa incredible time saver and marketing tool if you've built up even a small mailing list.

Benefits of using an autoresponder include:

- Sending out your ezine or newsletter and seeing how many people read it

- Organizing your email list by geographical area in order to target a specific state where you are performing

- Sending out a discount coupon for your CD or music download

- Ability to schedule when an email or newsletter is sent out

**119**

- Automatic notification to you when someone signs up

- Keeping track of click-thru rates and stats such as which links get clicked on the most

## PUTTING A WEB FORM ON SQUIDOO

Let's go through the process of putting a web form on Squidoo. Squidoo is a great place to gather up more people who can become loyal fans.

As mentioned before, your autoresponder will give you the HTML code for the form.

Once you have that code open up a blank word document. You can use any program, even a simple one like notepad. Paste this HTML code into the document. Do not add anything else or change this code.

Save document as "index.html"

Next, upload your document to your server. Here's an example:

If my domain is:

- http://www.myband.com

Then upload it as:

- http://www.myband.com/mailinglist/index.html

To make sure it is working, go to your browser and load the site with this address. The only thing you should see is the web form.

Next we need to get this into your Squidoo lens. You'll need to use the "Write" module for this. In the "Write" module paste this code:

```
<iframe src= "http://www.myband.com/mailing-
list/index.html" scrolling= "no" frameborder="no"
align="center" height="325px" width="325px"><br
/></iframe>
```

Replace the address above with the address that you uploaded the web form page to.

Save your lens and your web form will now show up on your lens.

If you're feeling a bit overwhelmed I can assure you that after you've done it once it will seem easy.

Autoresponders are an important tool that will help you organize your data and automate what you want to do with it. In addition, providing you with the code to easily make your web forms—and collecting the data—will benefit you as you build a mailing list of targeted fans.

Chapter 12
# ▸ YouTube

Along with MySpace, YouTube has changed the way people watch videos and communicate with each other. As a musician, you should seriously consider uploading video of live performances, practice sessions, or taped blogs in order to create a fan base on this social networking site.

People from all over the world go to YouTube to catch the latest videos. You will gain more exposure by uploading some video footage and attaching your web site to it. While most videos are short, they can be very beneficial to you in the long run.

## RATING SYSTEM

A huge driver to YouTube is people being able to rate their favorite videos and leave comments—text and video comments. These ratings are an important factor in determining the ranking of videos. The higher your ranking the more exposure you will receive. Similar to search engines, YouTube relies on number of searches and the popularity of a video to determine its ranking.

While you should be concerned about your ranking, I wouldn't worry about it too much. Using the strategies in this book will show you exactly how to drive traffic to any site, including YouTube. Just remember to tell people on your MySpace page and on your web site that you have video up on YouTube by providing a link or embedding the video on your page.

## ACTIVATING YOUR ACCOUNT

Signing up for a YouTube account is free and will only take a few minutes. Filling out the personal information forms and confirming your email address are all you will need to do. After opening an account, you will have to choose a username. This could be a little more complicated because of the number of subscribers. Choose a name that is easy to remember, but one that is not too common. You will be told if the username you choose is taken or not.

## VIDEO UPLOADING BASICS

Now you are ready to upload video. Before doing so, you should consider the following:

- Quality of your video. If you haven't made your video yet, you should keep in mind that you want the clearest picture possible. You may need to rent a camera that is capable of recording this type of video. If you know anyone who is able to shoot video, ask for their help. Viewers are fickle and they won't waste their time watching video that is difficult to see. With new technologies today, many home video cameras are very capable of shooting your video with fantastic results.

- According to YouTube video uploading guidelines, your video should not be longer than ten minutes and smaller then 100MB. If your video is too big, you can resize it during the editing process. Your video should also be in one of the following formats:

  - .WMV

  - .AVI

  - .MOV

  - .MPG

- The ideal specifications for your video as suggested by YouTube are:

  - MPEG4 (Divx, Xvid) format

  - 320x240 resolution

  - MP3 audio

  - 30 frames per second

- While you can record video using a cell phone, or web cam, the quality will not be as good. Keep this in mind before you begin shooting your video. If you have a strong subscriber base you can use these kind of videos for "Up to the minute" updates.

- Make sure the sound quality is clean before uploading. Viewers want to watch your video and hear your music.

- Always edit your video before uploading so you can make sure it is the right size and length. Keep it under five minutes as that seems to be the average.

- On YouTube, you will be able to upload as many video clips as you want. Video will remain on your account until you choose to remove it.

## VIDEO CONTENT

Be as creative as you can be with the content you upload. While a short video of your band performing is a great introduction, in order to maintain a fan base, you will have to be more creative in a future video. Content ideas include:

- Band bio (each band member says a little something about themselves)

- Music video using computer graphics, flip cards and other techniques

- Online blog or diary

- Funniest moments while performing

- Charity event or awards ceremony where your band is being featured or honored

- Band and fan interviews

- Rehearsal sessions

- Fan-made videos

- Music reviews of other artists

- Making-of video

- Question and Answer sessions

Try different formats and keep your fans guessing what you will do next. Creating video and uploading them can become addictive, so look at them as more than just a marketing tool and have some fun! If you have other talents besides music, why not incorporate them into your video?

## UPLOADING VIDEO

Uploading your video to YouTube is simple. There is an upload video button in the right hand corner of every page on YouTube. Click it and follow the instructions.

Choose a title, description, add tags, and include which category you want it to be featured in. Be descriptive and use deliberate keywords as this will make finding your video much easier.

Depending on how long your video is, it may take an hour or more. While most videos take only minutes, you have to take into consideration your connection speed, the number of videos that are being uploaded at the same time on YouTube, and the size of the video.

## OTHER YOUTUBE FEATURES

When you sign up for YouTube, you will be able to create your own groups and allow viewers to sign up to receive your new videos as soon as you upload them.

There are also widgets available that you can add to your MySpace profile page, and your web site so people can find your videos easily.

You will also be able to add your own list of favorites to your playlist, meet other musicians, and receive comments in your inbox.

As with other social networking sites, you will have to be proactive and diligent in uploading videos in order to receive a high rating. Since many people upload videos each day, your competition may be fierce, but it's well worth using YouTube as a way to increase your fan base and generate buzz about your sound.

## ACTIVE SHARING

When you use this feature, you will be able to let everyone know which videos you are watching and you will be able to see which videos others are watching. This can help you when building an email list or when trying to coax people to rate your own videos. You can do this by:

- Watching videos that are similar to yours and rating them

- Contacting people who have recently viewed a video that is similar to yours or the music you play and ask them to view your video

- Getting an idea of which videos are popular

- Seeing how many people view your own videos

- Increasing your email list by targeting those who have viewed your video

## ORDER OF VIDEOS

With this new feature, you will be able to choose the order in which you want your videos listed. This means if you want to create a series of videos, they will appear in the correct order.

Go to "my account" and click "Organize Videos."

You can create an archive of older videos by placing them further down on your list. This is a great feature that can help others find the videos you want to feature easier.

## UNBLOCKING USERS

You can now unblock users so they can view your profile page. Even though you should allow everyone to view your page so you can build a fan base, you may have accidentally blocked someone. Now you can unblock them.

# TESTTUBE

This is an area where you can play with new features that may be added to YouTube at some point. Current features include live chat and Audio-Swap.

AudioSwap will allow users to upload their videos with music from musicians that have a distribution contract with YouTube. This means that in the future, your music may appear on other users' videos.

Another feature being tested is called "Streams." This type of video allows users to chat in real-time as they watch it a video.

This could be a great marketing tool for musicians as you can use this type of video and audience interaction to launch a new CD or music download.

Instead of hosting a party via podcasting, you will be able to interact with fans and host a video launching party that includes feedback.

# ATTRACTING MORE FANS TO YOUR YOUTUBE PAGE

After opening your account, uploading a few videos, and creating a profile page, you cannot leave it to chance that you will be noticed on YouTube. Many aspiring musicians, artists, and others are vying for the attention of viewers, so competition is tough. Try some of the following suggestions, along with the other strategies in this book to help you achieve more recognition on YouTube:

- Subscribe to other musician profile pages and leave comments on their work. Not only will you be able to see how you compare with your competition, you will also increase your web presence by leaving your name in different places on YouTube.

- Start a YouTube group that discusses different aspects of music or the music industry in general. This will give you more exposure and also increase your web ranking because your name is attached to the group.

- Join existing groups and post comments whenever you can.

- Allow fans and others to embed your YouTube videos on their web sites, blogs, and profile pages on YouTube, MySpace, and Facebook. You can easily create an embeded icon that can be pasted to other web sites. This is a fun way for fans to show they care about your music.

- Create a link to your videos that fans can also use on their web sites or profile pages.

- Use podcasting as a way to televise live concerts. Many artists such as Sandi Thom and Terra Naomi broadcasted live or made video recordings of home concerts and were signed with major labels. Hold several small concerts in your home or other location every few days to entice new fans.

- Create a Vlog, which is an online blog and broadcast once or twice a week in addition to your usual blog. This is a great way to increase your fan base by allowing people into your personal space.

The most important way to increase your exposure on social networking sites like YouTube is by being a constant presence online. Join as many groups as you can, leave comments, and post new video, broadcast live, and give fans a reason to want to return to your page.

As changes continue to be made to YouTube, you will be able to have more control over uploading and getting your videos noticed by users and music executives. With YouTube, you have to be creative and create videos that are distinct if not downright innovative. This can only enhance your reputation as a musician and creative person. And remember, humor is always a great thing!

# Chapter 13
## ▶ RSS, Podcasts, and Internet Radio

## RSS FEEDS

RSS stands for "Really Simple Syndication" and is a format for delivering regularly changing web content. Many news-related sites, weblogs and other online publishers syndicate their content as an RSS Feed to whoever wants it.

The benefits of using RSS include:

- Keeps you informed by retrieving the latest content from sites you are interested in

- Saves time as you don't have to visit each site individually.

- Protects privacy as you can avoid having to sign up for a newsletter.

RSS feeds are growing rapidly. In order to read RSS you will need a feed reader or news aggregator that allows you to grab the RSS feeds from various sites and display them for you to read.

A variety of RSS Readers are available for different platforms such as:

- http://juicereceiver.sourceforge.net/index.php

- http://www.dopplerradio.net/

Many browsers such as Safari for Mac have an RSS reader built in. You'll see a small "RSS" button on the right inside the address bar when you are on a web site that offers an RSS feed. Click "RSS" and you'll be taken to the feed. On the right on the RSS page is an "Add Bookmark" link. Click that and you'll be subscribed and ready to receive updates from that feed. There are also a number of web-based feed readers available. My Yahoo, Google Reader, and Bloglines are popular web-based feed readers.

Once you have your Feed Reader, find sites that syndicate related content to your site and add their RSS feed to the list of feeds your Feed Reader checks. Many sites display a small icon with the acronyms RSS, XML, or RDF to let you know a feed is available.

You can also get an RSS Feed search generator that will seach for RSS Feeds based on keywords and automatically add new content to your site. Search engines will see this as updated content and they may rank you higher. Here's an example on how to do this in Squidoo.

## RSS FEEDS IN SQUIDOO LENSES

First you will need to get an RSS Feed link to insert in your module. You can get the link online by doing a search. The site we will be using is:

- http://www.rssfeedsgenerator.com

Go there and click on the link that says "News"

Select the services that you would like to receive news from such as "Google" "Yahoo" and "MSN" and then click "Next Step."

Type in a keyword related to your Squidoo lens subject. If you want to have more than one RSS feed, type in as many keywords as you want, one per line up to 10.

Highlight and copy the generated link.

Now go to your Squidoo account and edit your lens. In Squidoo, look for the "RSS Feeds" module. This module will allow you to insert frequently updated content from an RSS Feed link.

Click the "add modules" button, add the RSS module, then click the "Save" button.

Scroll down to the RSS Module and click "edit." Give your module a title.

In the URL box, paste the RSS feed URL you copied earlier. Select the module to update every 6 hours and leave the other options on default.

## WHAT ARE PODCASTS?

Simply put, podcasts are online audio content delivered via an RSS feed. You can listen to your podcasts on your computer with iTunes, Windows Media Player and others, or sync them with your iPod or other Mobile mp3 players and listen on the go. Podcasts are now also coming in the form of video.

In recent years, with the invention of portable music devices such as iPods, downloading music and broadcasting over the Internet has become popular with people of different generations. Because people are on the go more than ever, podcasting solves the problem of not being available when your favorite show is broadcast.

These radio shows have a continuous stream that allows the music to be played as it would on the radio, but is more convenient because listeners can listen anytime. Those with iPods or computers are able to subscribe to a podcast and listen to music mostly from unknown artists.

By uploading your tunes onto podcast music directories, such as the Podsafe Music Network at http://music.podshow.com/ your music will be picked up by those who run daily, weekly, and monthly podcasts. This is a great way to get your music heard by those who may not visit social networking sites.

There are about 3,000 podcasters listed in the music category on the Podcast Alley web site. Here's the link:

- http://www.podcastalley.com/

This site lists different podcasts that are available. Many podcasters have bi-weekly shows and need enough music to fill the time. This means the chance of your music being heard is better than excellent.

Since all podcasters have to list the songs they have chosen to play on Podcast Alley, you will know that your song is being played and how often. Also, many podcasters now work with satellite radio stations, which means your songs have a chance of reaching an even larger audience.

You can choose which songs you want to upload to the database. Whether you are promoting an upcoming CD or you just want one song to be played for now, the choice is yours. Once you upload a song, you are giving permission for it to be played at any time by any podcaster listed in the network. You can take your song down at any time and upload more songs if you choose. The best part is that this is a free service, so take advantage of this opportunity to expose your music.

## STANDING OUT TO PODCASTERS

With so many artists trying to get the attention of podcasters how can you get them to notice you? You might be surprised to discover that it is not necessarily doing something that has not been done before, but more often than not just doing the little things that other artists fail to do.

When the podcaster is deciding on what new songs to play, they will usually reward those who made their life a little easier and showed that they put some thought into it. Here are some helpful tips:

- Pay attention to the format of the podcaster that you are contacting.

- Personalize all correspondence. Never use "To whom it may concern" and then mention you love their show and listen all the time. If you had listened to their show you would know their name. Using a standard template is a good starting point but a personalized note will go a long way.

- Submit only to podcasts that are in genres relevant to your style of music. Do not submit to every podcast you know of, in hopes that they will play your music. Podcasters talk to each other and if you're bombarding everyone without regard to the focus of each podcast you won't be taken seriously.

It is important, just like in traditional radio, to create relationships. People like to work with people they feel good about. If your music is great and you develop these relationships the sky is the limit.

Treat podcasters just as special and important as you would traditional radio program directors and radio disc jockeys. After all they are that important and take a lot of time and effort to make these shows available.

Many traditional radio stations receive "Radio or Station IDs" from the artist they are playing. Why not do these with podcasters?

A station ID is simply a recorded voice tag line mentioning the radio station or podcaster. Provide the podcaster with a good quality recording of your voice alone. They can then mix your music in under your IDs or simply use it as an intro. Do not mix your song or anything else underneath your voice. Here are some examples:

> *"Hi this is Betty Bigtime of the band Bigtime Betty and your listening to our new song 'Todays the Day' on (insert name of podcaster)."*

> *"Hi this is Izzy Star and you're listening to (insert name of Podcaster)."*

> *"Hi this is Izzy Star of the Izzy Star Band and you're listening to my favorite podcast (insert name of Podcaster) with (insert host name)."*

> *"Hi this is Izzy Star, and I'm Drew Drummer, from the Izzy Star Band and you're listening to our favorite podcast (insert name of Podcaster). Go (insert podcast host name)."*

When you have finished these IDs you'll need to save them as Wave files or as mp3s. I do not recommend you forwarding them as attachments to the podcasters email unless you have first contacted the podcaster and received permission. Many times the email will go to the junk box because of the attachment and never be seen. A better idea is to provide a link they can click on to download the IDs. If you do not have a web site yet and can not provide a link you can try a service like:

- http://www.sendspace.com/

Here you can upload the file and they will send an email to the person with a link they can click to receive the file. It is better however, to have it from a domain you own as it gives your band a more professional appearance.

When a podcaster receives these station IDs they know that they are personalized specifically for them and no other podcaster can use them. This makes them feel extra special and important. It also demonstrates to them the following important things about you:

- You took the time to listen to their show

- You are conscious and respectful of their time

- You and your songs become more personal

- You respect what they're doing

Put your personality into your IDs and make sure they sound enthusiastic with lots of energy! There is nothing worse than receiving station id's and they sound like the person doing them was forced to do them or was sleeping.

Let them hear in your voice that you are excited about your music and being on their show. They usually play these right before they play your song to introduce your song.

Another good idea is to also make special station IDs for the big holidays such as Independence day, New Years and others.

## CHOOSING YOUR SONGS

When choosing songs for podcasts, you should follow the same rules as when you are uploading songs onto MySpace or other networking sites:

Choose songs you feel best represent your sound

- If songs are from a CD, choose one that best makes new fans want to hear more. This isn't always the best song on the CD

- Rotate your songs so that a few are on the podcasting network

- Include live or acoustic versions of your songs as they will be played by different podcasters

- If there is a particular song that everyone seems to be strongly reacting to, choose that one. Just make sure you have more great songs to follow up with!

## UPLOADING YOUR SONGS

It is easy to upload your songs to the Podsafe Music Network.

The first step is to register yourself or your band. Fill out all relevant information. Write a short bio about your band and your latest gigs, music, CDs, and other info podcasters want to know. You have the option of leaving a little note about music promotion. Mention your web site and provide all URLs, blog, or other marketing ventures you are involved in.

After reading the web site disclaimer, you can begin uploading your songs.

Since the network lists the song you upload last first on its playlist, it is important to consider the order in which you want your songs to appear. Upload one or two songs to start. See if they catch on and then upload more. This is a good way to see which podcasters are interested in your music.

Other things to consider:

- **Upload full songs only**

  Podcasters do not want to play portions of songs. In addition full songs will have a greater chance of being noticed since you will be getting more "Play Time."

- **Make sure you upload all songs in mp3 file format**

  Podcasters can only broadcast in this format. Upload your songs at 128kbps so they can be streamed properly when broadcasted.

- **Do not include spaces in your music title**

  Stick to the standard way of naming an mp3 file. Example: john_public-imastar.mp3. Although this is becoming less of a issue, it is better to be safe.

- **Create an ID3 tag**

  This is so your file can be traced back to your web site and provide any additional information the podcaster might want to use while broadcasting. What better way to gain free publicity than having a podcaster announce your latest music, CD, gig, or other event? You can imbed this information using Windows Media Player or iTunes very easily. In Windows Media Player upload your song into the media player and right click on the file name. Choose "Advance Tag Editor." You will be sent to a menu that contains empty boxes where you can insert information. In iTunes simply select the song and go to "get info" menu or hit command I. Fill out any relevant boxes, save your song and upload it to the Podsafe Music Network.

- **Play it back and check it**

  The final step is to play your song back before uploading it to make sure there aren't any issues with the recording. There is nothing worse than uploading a song that sounds awful or is even the wrong song or version of a song, because you failed to double check and correct any mistakes.

- **Verify all contact information**

Once you get the hang of uploading songs and providing all the information necessary to get a podcaster's attention, you will begin to build a reputation among the podcasters. It is important to always be professional and treat podcasters with respect as they can choose to overlook future songs if you are rude or insensitive.

Use podcasting as a way to build your fan base and attract attention from music labels. There are many podcasts in need of music and new ones are created each day. It's a free and excellent tool to spread the word about your music.

There are many ways musicians can use podcasting to attract new fans, record executives and booking agents. Use podcasts to:

- Showcase different genres you are capable of performing in.

- Upload live tracks as well as recorded tracks to show your band's diversity.

- Upload extended versions of songs that showcase certain instruments.

- Ask podcasters, once you have developed a relationship with them, to announce songs that are featured on your new CD and where people can purchase it.

You should add podcast information to your web site, so visitors will be able to listen when they want. If you have a new CD, let people know where they will be able to hear the full versions of songs from it.

## INTERNET RADIO

In addition to podcasts, those who produce Internet radio shows are also in need of good music. Two places to find Internet radio shows are:

- LIVE365.com: http://www.live365.com

- SHOUTcast.com: http://www.shoutcast.com

Find webcasts that fit your genre and read more about how to submit your music. Getting a response quickly is the hardest part of this process, which is why you should submit music to at least twenty or thirty webcasts. If you don't get a response after a few weeks, contact the program director and ask about the status of your CD or single.

While this process can take a month or more, once your music is being played on these webcasts, it will become more popular with other webcasts.

If you want to start your own webcast, you can do so easily. This will give your music a chance to be heard right away after you open an account on one of the web sites mentioned above.

There are many benefits to starting your own webcast including:

- The ability to add links to the webcast on your web site, MySpace profile page, Facebook page, Squidoo lenses, newsletter, and any other place you advertise your music.

- The ability to leave messages on forums, chat with people about your webcast, and write press releases advertising it.

- The ability to play any types of music you want, which means if you have musician friends, you can help them out.

- The ability to market your music and upcoming events.

- The ability to create a webcast site that includes back links to all other marketing sites you have.

There are thousands of people who subscribe to Internet radio shows each month, so you will quickly find devoted fans. Running a webcast is fun and does not take much time. It also offers you a chance to reach many people each month.

# Chapter 14
## ► Facebook

Facebook is an online social network that attracted college age users at first because it was marketed as a place to upload resumes, find people, and build work-related contacts. While the site is still used for these purposes, users can now upload photos, video, connect their web site and other profile pages, and join in hundreds of forums and online groups.

Recently Facebook changed their registration restrictions and the site currently has 26.6 million unique U.S. visitors, a result that suggests Facebook's decision to drop registration restrictions was a good one. Facebook saw an 89% increase in U.S.-based visitors in May 2007 compared with the same period the previous year, according to Internet metrics firm ComScore.

Comparing May 2006 to May 2007, Facebook also saw its average number of monthly page views jump from 6.5 billion to 15.8 billion, a 143% increase. In addition, the average number of minutes spent on the site per visitor per month also increased, rising from 138 to 186 on average, a 35% increase. This should be enough to convince you of the importance of using Facebook in your music marketing campaigns.

If you are looking for another vehicle to access fans, make connections with music producers, other musicians, and others who may be able to help your career, creating a Facebook account is something to consider.

## CREATING YOUR ACCOUNT

Facebook is another free service and registration is easy. Follow the prompts and you're done. After creating your account, you should create a profile. This will be how friends and others will find you. Your profile can include any information you want it to. If you are using Facebook to promote your music, you should include the following:

- Name
- Band name
- Your web site
- Your location
- Photos

- Local hangouts

- Recent gigs and events

- Upcoming events

These items will help people learn more about you and your band.

After registering, you will be asked about your security preferences. This site offers you more control over who sees your pages than others. While you want people to find out more about you, you should also limit some of your content to friends only. This will make them feel special and prompt others to join your list so they can see additional pictures and video.

## BENEFITS OF A HOMEPAGE

Your homepage is where you will find news about others in your group of friends or groups you belong to. This means that when you have news to share, it will end up on their homepages as well. This is a great way to create a viral marketing campaign within the Facebook community. Homepages also include newsfeeds that include information about others on the site, notifications, and alerts when an important date comes up.

In 2006, Facebook added a live newsfeed option to its profile pages that allowed users to upload information, photos, and other items so everyone on their group list would receive it. While many users were upset that this option had been created, for musicians, this was another way to create a viral marketing campaign without having to email everyone in the group.

Newsfeeds and minifeeds can help you spread the word about upcoming gigs, new releases of your music, and much more. Use them to highlight certain events that are taking place such as new videos, the formation of a new group, or the creation of a blog.

## UPLOADING PHOTOS AND VIDEO

Uploading photos and sharing them with people is another way to generate interest. Once you have created a profile, you can begin building a friends list. Whenever you upload photos, you can have them sent directly to your friends. You can upload video as well.

## LINKING YOUR BLOG

You also have the option of linking your blog to your Facebook page. This is a great way to get others interested in your music. Instead of having to create a separate blog, connecting it will save time and increase your web ranking. The more web sites that have links to your web site, the higher your ranking will be.

# FACEBOOK GROUPS

One of the most effective ways to create a friends list is by joining some groups. There are many to choose from, so join ones that interest you. You will be able to chat with other musicians and those who are interested in the same types of music you are. This is also a good place to announce your new CD or web site.

Facebook groups are different from other groups found on YouTube and MySpace in that the atmosphere is more mellow and you will find more professional people have accounts than those who are just looking to become famous quickly.

If you don't have time to create a group on Facebook, why not have fans create one for you? Fans enjoy being part of a musician's success. Fans also enjoy talking about your upcoming gigs and new videos.

Many times choosing a fan or a friend to moderate your group will help it become more successful. Encourage fans to post photos from your concerts, create blogs about their experiences, and encourage them to spread the word about your music by mentioning you on their own profile pages.

# CREATING FLYERS

A flyer is a special advertisement that you can use to advertise on local college boards. If you have an upcoming gig, you can place flyers on all the schools within your area. Many college students use these boards to find stuff to do on the weekends or during the week.

Flyers cost five dollars and can be displayed 2,500 times on the school board of your choice and on Facebook pages of those who attend that school. You will be notified about the number of flyers you currently have out and they will be distributed by Facebook until they are gone.

You can also post flyers on various school boards, but you must purchase separate flyers for each school.

You can include basic information about your gig, upload a photo, and add your web site URL.

In order to purchase a flyer, fill out the simple form provided and make sure all the information is correct as you will not be given the opportunity to change anything once you pay for the flyer.

You can use flyers to:

- Promote your new CD and music

- Advertise any school events you may be participating in

- Let people know you have a web site

This is a fun feature that allows you to target specific groups of people.

## FACEBOOK APPS

Another new feature recently introduced by Facebook allows companies to advertise on profile pages. You will be able to choose from a list of apps that can be applied to your page.

Benefits of including apps on your page:

- Promote other social networking sites you have profile pages on

- Place affiliate links so you can earn cash. For example, in the future, we might allow affiliates to sell this book. When someone buys it you can receive a commission as high as 70% simply for advertising the links on your pages

- Increase your web ranking on Facebook by including company apps on your page

- Attract different groups of people who are interested in the products offered on your page

New apps will be displayed in your news feed which is sent to those on your friends list. This is a brand new feature and there are currently only 30 apps to choose from. Many more are expected to be added. MySpace is beginning to limit the amount of widgets you can add to your profile page, so this is an exciting development.

## FACEBOOK MOBILE

Facebook mobile is now available so people can download songs, photos, and other items to their cell phones and PDAs. This a another feature you can take advantage of when marketing your music. Upload songs, video, and photos to encourage people to download them to their mobile devices. They can create ringtones, wallpaper, and receive updates on their newsfeed.

## WHY YOU SHOULD JOIN FACEBOOK

This social networking site should be used to find social career connections in addition to increasing your fan base and building a viral buzz. While you will attract those who enjoy your music, you should also join groups in order to meet people that are interested in furthering your career and those that you can help as well through these new found connections.

Facebook is the sixth most viewed site on the Internet. While it began as a site that helped connect college students, those who have graduated are still using the site, which means that it continues to grow. As a musician, you want to appeal to many different groups of people. Most Facebook users are in their mid-to-late-twenties and are very interested in the music scene. This is a great chance for you to share your experiences, plug your music, and gain more exposure.

## Chapter 15
▸ **Winning Fans With A Blog**

Over the last few years, blogging has really taken off. Take a look around the World Wide Web and you're never more than a couple of clicks away from a new blog. They're being created at a rapid rate and their popularity continues to grow.

Blogging has had a serious effect on the future of news broadcasting in terms of what and when news is spread and by whom.

In this chapter we'll be looking at the effect of blogging. I'll explain how MySpace's blogging features can be put to good  use as a way to stay connected to fans and reach more markets online. Keep in mind there are many other places to create a blog.

Very few trends have taken off as quickly as blogging. Many times, you see it without even noticing. Winning fans with a blog is a proven technique and by the end of this chapter you should be capable of putting one to good use.

## WHAT IS A BLOG?

Blogs can take on many different styles, but most of them are used as a form of personal journal or cyber diary.

By creating a blog, you have a direct utility to publish content on the web. It's a form of self-publication. What you choose to write about is entirely up to you.

You could blog about your travels and experiences around the country. You could write a short story on your neighbor's eating habits. It really doesn't matter.

Blogging gives you the opportunity to voice your opinions, however weird and wonderful they may be, and gives other people the opportunity to read them.

This has resulted in a massive shift in web content. Whereas previously, most stories came from professional journalists, we now have a situation where the power is with the people.

Most blogs work in simple fashion. You have a host that broadcasts your blog over the Internet.

The host will provide a posting interface that lets you add entries, along with a few other basic options, like adding links to your web site, video blogging, and adding photos to make your blog more interesting.

You should of course create a MySpace blog, and you may also want to create a separate blog at one of the sites below:

- Wordpress

- Blogger

- eblogger

Each of these hosts will provide you with the options mentioned above. With these blogs, you will be able to create back links to your web site and to your MySpace blog, Facebook, and YouTube. Also check with your web host to see if blogs come with your monthly fee.

Your blogs comes with a fully-fledged commenting system. One of the best things about posting your thoughts is that other people can come along and agree or disagree with them. Don't worry if people disagree with your opinions, it will make your blog more interesting. It's better for people to disagree than to say nothing at all.

Through your MySpace blog, you can control the comments people post, but if you want to start a great discussion and have people respond to comments posted, then you should allow all comments to be seen.

## OTHER TYPES OF BLOGS

As mentioned above, in addition to creating a blog on MySpace, you can create a blog on your web site, or sign up for a blog space on sites like Blogger. These blogs are sometimes easier to market than blogs created on MySpace as there are still many people though many people not on MySpace. Catering to this segment of the population is just as important as catering to those who frequent social networking sites.

Common types of blogs you may see on the Internet include:

- Business or industry blogs

- News blogs

- Personal blogs

- Promotional blogs

Depending on the type of personality you have and what you want to blog about, any of these can help your career.

## BUSINESS OR INDUSTRY BLOGS

These blogs are very specific in nature. If you want to create a blog that informs people about the music industry, helps other struggling musicians, or informs those who may not be familiar with technological advances in the music industry, then this is the type of blog you can create. While these blogs can be personal in nature, they are not as personal as diary-type blogs. Include a lot of pertinent information and update frequently.

## NEWS BLOGS

A news blog can be about anything that is going on in the news. If you are a news junky, then this is the type of blog for you. Scour the news web sites, read the newspaper, and report what you read that is of interest to those who have visited your site. You can focus on a certain segment or the population or you can write about a wide variety of topics. Offer commentary, humor, and other items you feel will attract readers.

## PERSONAL BLOGS

These blogs are used to tell your story. Many blogs of this nature are found on MySpace. Write about your days as a musician, upcoming gigs, and other information fans would be interested in reading about.

## PROMOTIONAL BLOGS

These blogs are specifically created to alert fans and others about what is going on in your music career. If you are releasing new music, promoting upcoming gigs, or announcing that you've signed a recording contract, this is the type of blog you will want to write. Less personal in nature, this blog is about your music career and goals only.

I can't tell you which blog to create, but I can tell you that you should definitely create one. Blogs are a way for people to connect with you. People you make a connection with are more likely to listen to your songs, buy your music or CD, and hear you play live.

## SETTING UP YOUR MYSPACE BLOG

Unlike other blogging applications, you don't have to worry about installing any software to post your thoughts on MySpace.

All of the features you'll need are already in place. You can be up and running with a brand new blog in a matter of minutes.

- Go to your main MySpace account homepage.

- From the list of options, select "Manage Blog."

- This takes you to the blogging interface, which will be empty until you start adding your entries.

When you post your first entry, it will appear in the right hand pane. You will also be shown new posts from blogs that you're subscribed to. Every MySpace blog has the option to subscribe to future posts. This can be a very handy tool. It lets you build a type of mailing list. The more people you have subscribed to your blog, the more people your entries are automatically posted to.

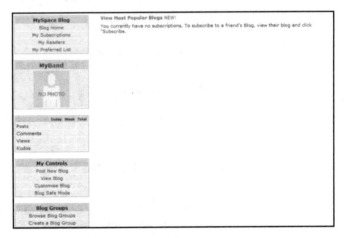

*The MySpace blogging interface*

The above screenshot illustrates what a new blog will look like. Let's have a look at the options that are available to you by default.

- **Blog Home**

  This is the link to the page that you're currently viewing.

- **My Subscriptions**

  This keeps track of your current subscriptions. You can sort through the current listings and cancel blogs that you no longer wish to receive updates from. I'd strongly recommend that you subscribe to blogs from similar artists. Not only will it give you a good idea of what other people are doing with their blogs, your name will appear in their "My Readers" list. This often encourages them to give your own entries a read. People like to know about the readers they're attracting. You will also attract the attention of the readers of these blogs. People will often check out the blogs of those posting comments to see what they have to say on other topics.

- **My Readers**

  When somebody subscribes to your blog, they will be listed on

this page. You'll also be able to see the date that they subscribed. Keep a close eye on your readers. Is there a trend? Are
you attracting a certain group of people? The more readers you
have, the better it is for your marketing campaign. MySpace
users rarely subscribe to random blogs. If you do get regular
readers, don't let them sit there! Make them your priority targets
for new advertising campaigns. They've already stated their
interest in what you have to say, so if you've got a new record on
the way, it makes sense to tell them about it.

- **My Preferred Readers**

    You can choose to limit access to your blog to people on your
    preferred list. While this may be a good idea for users with
    personal interests to discuss, you are not on MySpace to talk
    about your personal life. You're here to publicize your music.
    Always allow full access to your blog. Further down the page,
    you'll see a small block with statistics for posts, comments,
    kudos, and views. Posts, comments, and views are straightfor-
    ward. Kudos are added to your account when somebody likes an
    entry and gives you them. They can add one or two, depending
    on how strongly they like your piece. If you're getting kudos, it's
    generally a good sign. It can be misleading too, however. Some
    people will give them as an incentive for you to visit their own
    blog and return the favor.

- **Post New Blog**

    We will look at this in greater detail later in the chapter.

- **View Blog**

    This link takes you to an overview of your blog entries.

- **Customize Blog**

    The blog customization settings are extremely handy. By adjust-
    ing the options, you can re-skin how your blog will look. It's pos-
    sible to change a number of default settings, including:

    - Header

    - Font and text size

    - Background color

    - Personal details displayed alongside the blog

    - Background music

    - Layout of the modules

It's a good idea to play around with your blog until you get a look that
compliments your profile template. Don't make it outrageously unortho-
dox. The best blogs are always the ones where the focus is on the
writing itself.

- **Blog Safe Mode**

  You can test your blog for errors by entering safe mode and replacing stray HTML code.

- **Browse Blog Groups**

  Many people choose to add groups to their blogs. It is similar to creating a circle of friends. Your blog is placed in a category and you can boost your exposure within that group.

- **Create Blog Group**

  If you're feeling particularly creative, you can create your own blog group. This is great if you have a unique selling point, or a special niche, but it's not necessary. Some of the best blogs are independent from affiliation and networks.

## ADDING A NEW ENTRY

To add a new entry to your blog, follow the "Post New Blog" link.

You'll now see a screen resembling the screenshot on the next page.

As you can see, there are plenty of options to customize and it's possible to take full control of what the user will see when they access your page.

The main body of the blog consists of a WYSIWYG editor.

WYSIWYG simply stands for What You See Is What You Get. It's a form of editor developed primarily for users who don't have a grasp of HTML coding.

Thankfully, the WYSIWYG editor takes care of this problem by translating our input data into HTML code.

That's not to say that HTML can't be used, however. If you do happen to know a few tags, they can be placed inside the text area and they'll produce the desired effect.

For our purposes, you shouldn't need them too often. Blogging is more about what you have to say than the format that it's presented in.

A quick word of advice: If you're going to post a lengthy blog, always remember to save it in a standard word document beforehand. If the site or your browser crashes before you can post, you're going to be frustrated at having to start over from the beginning. Write your post in a Word document or the like and then cut and paste it into your blog.

*The Post New Blog screen*

Here's a rundown of the functions used to post your first blog.

- **Post Date**

  This will automatically set itself. But if you wish to change it to a date in the past, it's possible. Perhaps more interestingly, you can set a date in the future for your blog to be posted.

- **Post Time**

  Similarly, you can alter the time for when the blog should go live.

- **Subject**

  Try to think of something intriguing for your blog title. Make your piece sound as interesting as possible. Many blogs rely on catchy titles to draw traffic from news-feed web sites. Without a title that stands out, the link will be missed entirely.

- **Category**

  Always state a category for your entry. This is so it can be placed in the correct sub-section of the blogging community. Users will often search for new blogs to read. If you're in the wrong section, you're not going to be attracting the right readers. Choose the category that's most relevant to your content.

- **Body**

  This is where the main content of the entry goes. Be careful if you're pasting from a word document. Programs like Microsoft Word tend to throw in lots of extra formatting code, and this can make your entry look somewhat contorted. You can check for stray formatting by selecting the "View Source" box. This will display the HTML output.

- **Tell Us What You're Listening To**

  You can search through the MySpace catalogues to announce to the world what you're currently listening to.

- **Current Mood**

  Choose your current mood, complete with matching MySpace emoticon.

- **Comments**

  You can opt to disable kudos and comments by selecting this box. I wouldn't recommend it, however. But you may find an occasion where you want to say what's on your mind without dealing with the comments that follow.

- **Privacy**

  Make your entries public. You're here to expand your network. You won't gain anything by limiting your blogs to those who you've already added to your friends list.

- **Podcast Enclosure**

  If you have a podcast to go with the entry, post it here.

Now click the "Preview and Post" option. You'll be shown how your blog will appear. If you're satisfied, confirm the post and it will be added to your blog.

If you have set a posting date or time in the future, it will be added at that particular date or time.

## THE FUTURE OF NEWS REPORTING

Did you know that by 2020, it's expected that 50% of the world's news will be reported by individual bloggers?

News stations are picking up on blogs and reporting them as they would with any other source. They are also including blogs on their web sites.

The result is that we have a brilliantly diverse stage for news to be presented to the world. Opinions can now circulate without having to be approved by a newspaper editor.

There are many blogging networks offering platforms for independent writers to present their ideas and opinions to the world. These networks have grown so expansive that they've become some of the most visited web sites on the net. Information is taken directly from blogs and sent on to media stations.

In the past, blogs were reactionary information sources. The media reported something, then the web community wrote about it. These days, that same community is providing stories to the national press.

## SPREADING A VIRAL BUZZ

A viral buzz can be the highpoint of your MySpace marketing campaign. It can be the making of ANY marketing campaign.

Many would go as far as to say that it's the future of marketing altogether. But what is it?

When I talk about a viral buzz, I'm alluding to the public interest around a certain subject. Viral buzz is publicity spread via word of mouth using email, blogs, and social networking sites.

If I tell you that so-and-so has an incredible album coming out and you pass the information on to somebody else, a viral buzz is being created. It's manipulating the trust that friends place in each other, to promote a cause through non-biased means.

Traditionally, advertisements have been placed between television shows, on the radio or maybe even plastered on a towering billboard. They can be effective but there is a lot of competition. And with the world moving at 100,000 miles per hour, people are tuning out most of what they believe to be pure advertising. Advertisements are brilliant when you're promoting a product that no one else has. If you can expose a new concept or a new idea that forces people to sit up and take notice, you'll achieve a great deal of success.

But most of the time, advertising agencies are competing with each other. To be effective advertising in a commercial break, you have to be able to outshine your competition.

The trouble is when competition levels are so high and so much information is coming at people in every direction, people can't make their mind up one way or the other. At this point, what becomes the primary influence? Is it the slogan at the end of the advertisement? The colors used? No, it's something far different. The customer will decide based on positive reviews given by friends, family and other direct influences.

Trends and fashion are reliant on word of mouth to determine what's in and what's out. If you can get people talking about you, you're going to receive exposure.

Whether the resulting publicity is positive or negative will depend largely on whether you can back up your claims.

But how does this affect blogging?

If you're a canny blogger, it's possible to get people talking about what you have to say. The most obvious method is through the commenting system. If users are intrigued by what you have to say, they'll let you know about it.

The second way is when you can garner publicity is through external links. Not everybody using MySpace is restricted to MySpace alone. Many journalists and web authors scour blogs looking for information and opinions that they can use in their news stories.

To generate a viral buzz, here are some of the possibilities to consider:

- Write about political and potentially explosive issues.

- Write informative pieces other people can benefit from. Maybe you have advice to help others write better songs? Maybe you can help them get started?

- Humor and comedy. Do you have a good time on the road? Can you recount experiences that would amuse readers? Tell your stories—it helps people relate to you.

- Take an interest in a good cause. Becoming an active part of a charity and send out good vibes about your intentions. It might sound a bit false, but it makes a difference to your brand image.

The idea is to encourage people to listen to what you have to say. Keep an eye on the number of people that are subscribed to your blog. If the number continues to increase, you're doing something right.

## GRABBING CONTACT DETAILS

If you're running a blog that provides useful information, tips or advice, here's a great way to capture your target audience and keep them in your grasp: take their contact details.

You can do this by asking them to send their details as a "subscription" via the messaging system.

Of course, you can't go against your word. If you're going to take your friends' contact details, you'll need to provide them with what you specified. But their contact details can also be used to form an extensive mailing list of people who are particularly likely to buy in to your word.

To be good at marketing, you should never say no to an extra contact, even if you can't find an immediate use for it.

## WHAT TO WRITE ABOUT

For many people, writing a blog is scary because they don't know what to write about or how to go about writing it. Depending on the type of blog you want to write, you should always consider the following in order to make your blog more popular.

- Make sure your blog is grammatically correct. Blogs that have spelling errors will not be taken seriously.

- Include topics that both entertain and entice people into reading future blogs. Your topics may be music related if you want them to be, but you can write about anything as long as it interests you.

- Update your blog often so people will want to return. If you only post once every few weeks, you will lose people quickly.

- Keep your posts between 150 and 300 words. People do not want to read for more than five minutes or so.

- Include useful information that readers will find interesting. This will keep readers wanting more.

## FINAL WORD ABOUT BLOGS

If you don't like to write, then you may want to get someone else to write your blog for you or you should keep your blog as short as possible. Readers will be able to tell if you aren't interested in writing a blog. They will not want to return to read more of your posts and the blog will become a waste of time.

If you aren't comfortable writing a blog, but you want to, visit other blogs that are popular to learn how. Most blogs are conversational in tone and are non-threatening to readers. Once you write a few entries, you will begin to develop your own unique style that readers will recognize and appreciate.

Chapter 16
# ▸ Selling Music On Your Own

As you learned before, selling your own music online can be lucrative. Use social networking sites to help increase your sales.

Many independent artists have found the opportunity with the emergence of the digital music era to make a very good profit with their music. Some have even quit their day jobs and work on what they love full time.

Over the course of this chapter, I'm going to focus on how you can sell your own music without the help of a record label.

It's possible to distribute music made in your bedroom to a worldwide audience, such is the power of the Internet.

# THE ADVANTAGES OF BEING INDEPENDENT
## MAKING YOUR OWN DECISIONS

When you decide not to pursue or sign a recording contract, you have more freedom in creating and marketing your music.

From the music to the cover art, you control all angles and promotion strategies. And to the delight of many independent artists you'll keep all the profit.

### Flexibility

When producing an album yourself, you can take as long as you need. If good ideas aren't flowing freely you can walk away from the project without the phone ringing and a concerned manager asking for a status report.

### CUTTING DOWN COSTS

Twenty years ago, the idea of releasing music without a label was difficult at best. Few artists could afford to produce an album and pay for all the marketing involved.

These days, you can strike up deals with third party distribution web sites and have your music accessible to the world. The only thing you have to worry about is promoting the music yourself and this book is showing you exactly how to do that.

It doesn't have to be digital either. There are still distribution companies that specialize in taking your music and cover art, packaging it from scratch, and forwarding it on to the people who are willing to buy it.

I'd recommend that if you're going to sell your music, you start out by working with those who have solid reputations.

Some download merchants will host your music for free, if you're willing to pay a percentage of commission on any sales that you make. Some are aggregators, and will get your music on all the big digital sites like iTunes and simply take a percentage, a setup fee or both.

## RELEASING MUSIC IN DIGITAL FORMAT

The boom of the Internet has created opportunities for releasing your music independently widely available across the Net. Need further proof?

Here's a list of the many businesses offering retail advice, and services for your music.

- 96 Decibels

- Apollo Tunes

- Arkada

- Artistopia

- Audigist

- Amazon Advantage

- Artists First

- Audiolunchbox

- Bebo

- CafePress (Offers additional merchandising services)

- CD Baby

- CD Fuse

- CD Unsigned

- CD WOW

- Channel 4 Music

- Download

- Earbuzz
- EmuBands
- Epic Tunes
- Ijamr
- Indie Rhythm
- IntoMusic
- Isound
- Last.fm
- Lulu
- Magnatune
- Masscharts
- M-deck
- Mperia
- Musicforte
- Music Freedom
- Mvine
- Mymusicstream
- Netunes
- NME
- Payplay.com
- PureVolume
- Second Life
- Soundclick
- Tagets
- Totalband
- Trackseller
- Tradebit
- Tunecore
- Tunetribe
- UBL
- The Weed Files

URLs can change so I'd recommend running a Google search for the name of the business. This will take you to their most up-to-date sites.

As you can see, there are MANY service providers on the market. Some, such as Café Press, come with additional features enabling you to open an entire online store including merchandise such as t-shirts.

They'll even print and ship your merchandise to customers for a commission on sales.

Virtual reality sites like Second Life are another inventive marketing tap. By signing up on Second Life, you enter a completely authentic virtual world where it's possible to sell your work and socialize with other so-called Second Lifers.

As you can see, the possibilities are endless. Take advantage of as many as possible in order to promote your music.

## MARKETING ON THE MOVE

Much of this book has discussed ways to promote your work online, whether it's through the haven of MySpace or a third party retail web site. It's important to remember that the best marketing campaigns are very much adapted to exploit as many rewarding avenues as possible.

Marketing on the move is fundamental to your success.

What I mean by this is that you should never be too far away from your sales pitch. There are marketing opportunities all around us, and if you don't keep your eyes peeled, you could miss out on many ways to market your music.

When you switch off your computer and head out for a night on the town, you should feel entitled to a good time. But treat every social experience as a possible showcase for your work. I'm not saying you should rattle off slogans and catchphrases like a robotic lunatic. But many sales people grab customers in the least likely of situations.

Then there are also the more obvious situations.

If you're playing a gig at a local bar, or anywhere for that matter, don't let the fans leave without learning where to find you online. Have somebody hand out fliers at the event and ALWAYS ensure that your MySpace or web site URL is listed. If the people in attendance enjoy your performance, they're likely to check out the web site. It doesn't mean that they'll purchase a record, but many people will add you just to say "Great show last night" or something equally rewarding and innocuous.

In addition to flyers, you can also:

- Create a hand stamp to be used at your shows that features your web site

- Hang up banners that include your band name and web site

- Always include your web site on CDs you are selling

- Hand out business cards whenever possible with your web URL

- Post business cards on community bulletin boards in restaurants, laundromats, and grocery stores

- Place your band name and web address on any other merchandise you sell or hand out

Any leaflets, contact cards or email should be accompanied by the all important MySpace URL or your web site address.

Get into a frame of mind where your MySpace homepage, and other social networking sites you belong to, are other methods of staying in touch. You can use them to promote your work without even making the first move.

Scout around the local pubs and bars. Is there any way you can get a poster up to advertise an upcoming show? If you can, it's a great way of getting exposure amongst the people who are likely to attend such events.

You can even plug the URL in your mobile phone voicemail!

Likewise, any email that you send to your friends should have a signature attached. In this signature, place your URL as a hyperlink. Spreading the word as widely as possible is imperative to your success.

If there's a band playing locally, and you feel that your music is the same style, head out there with fliers and wait at the doors after the show. It's a good idea to speak to the management beforehand, but once you're there, the benefits are many.

Targeting fans in such a way is likely to get your name out there with the people that really matter.

It's important to lose the mindset that social networking sites are the only places you can advertise your music. They're not. People you talk to offline are likely to visit your web site or profile page once you mention it.

## THE NEW MYPURCHASE SYSTEM

MySpace has announced that it will soon be integrating a download store where users will be able to purchase music through its web site.

This is a large step forward and one which has been greeted by mixed feelings from the music community.

The system will allow the downloading of single MP3s, and a commission will be taken from each sale. As of yet, these details have been kept under close wrap.

For the independent scene, such a system represents great reason for optimism. It won't be long until you're able to add songs to MySpace and set a "purchase" option alongside the usual settings.

Many artists have openly questioned the commissions that MySpace will be making as the provider of this service. But there is no doubt that this is an incredible opportunity to build up your fans and let them buy your music instantly and easily. The path of least resistance is always best, and this is as easy as it gets to find new artists and music to purchase. While many artists deeply resent the idea of their concept albums being fragmented in to single mp3s it is clear that the public is at the moment very "Hit Single" oriented.

It remains to be seen whether the MyPurchase system will take off, but signs are promising, especially if you're on the lookout for a service which moulds social networking with a secure paid download utility.

To put things in perspective, iTunes sells songs at 99 cents. Of this, the artist receives 70 cents and the remaining 29 cents is paid to iTunes as commission for using the service.

The MyPurchase system will probably cost around the same for each download. The commissions should be comparable as well.

If you are selling music through other online means, you do not have to participate in this new program. You might want to save your MySpace page so new visitors will be able to sample your music for free.

## LAST MINUTE PROMOTION

If you've settled on a release date for a record that you plan to sell, the 24 hours prior to the record going on sale, marketing wise, are very important.

Last minute promotion is a key element to your success, and it'll give a tremendous boost to your opening sales.

Go out and arrange a party for the night before your record goes on sale. Hosting a great social event and showcasing some of your material in an environment that people are going to enjoy is a great way to promote your product by.

You can even tease the fact that the party is special by selling your work as a "Pre-Release" at the event, along with any other merchandise. You can also host an online launch party by setting up a podcast or streaming video of the event. Offering CDs and downloads at a discount price for one night only will increase overall sales. This is a unique idea where you can invite total strangers on the Internet to enjoy your success.

Announce your launch party on your MySpace calendar and on other social networking sites. Invite a few friends over, make sure your web site can take orders, and broadcast your party live. You can also create video from pictures taken or create a vlog after the event.

It's a good idea to spread the word as widely as possible. Try to grab a local radio appearance on the eve of the release, or arrange a press release for any local newspapers that would be willing to follow the story. You can also write your own press release and distribute it all over the Internet. There are also press release sites such as:

- http://www.prweb.com/

There are many journalists looking for these leads. Why? It makes their jobs ten times easier for one thing. They don't like to have to scout out every story and you can give them a helpful nod in the direction of your own news.

Local advertising shouldn't be overlooked however, even if you're appealing to an international audience on social networking sites.

## CROSS-PROMOTIONAL SUCCESS ON MYSPACE

So what about that international audience? Whether you're selling your record digitally or as a CD there's a lot of money to be made with cross-promotion.

Take a good look around MySpace and keep an eye on any artists who happen to be releasing records in the not too distant future.

If they're releasing a record, it's likely that they're going to be using the same marketing venues you will be using.

So why not do each other a favor?

Striking up a deal to promote somebody else's work as well as your own is a brilliant way of rapidly expanding the circle of people that are likely to take an interest in your record—as long as they offer the same in return, of course.

If you can arrange a deal with several artists, this process becomes even more effective. People will begin to catch on and see mentions of your record in different places. Constant brand exposure is a likely way to bring you sales from curious and casual fans alike.

# Chapter 17
## ▸ A Simple Craigslist Strategy

Here's a strategy that works very quickly. I don't know the exact reasons why but for some reason the San Francisco Bay Area Craigslist is indexed extremely fast by Google and is a great way to drive extra traffic to your site. This also works with a similar site called Backpage. These sites are basically online classified advertisements.

The best place for these ads is in the "sm biz ads" in the "services" section as it will be easier to write an ad that wont be flagged as much. You can also try other music categories. Just make sure your ads sound like they belong there.

Write a headline using your most popular keywords. Then continue writing the main part of your classified advertisement. Make sure to include your keywords in the ad and to put a link to your site or Squidoo lens. It's important that it does not sound like you are spamming or you will get flagged and they will delete your ad. You could mention your free ebook here as well.

The goal of this strategy is to send more people to your web site or Squidoo lens. Unless you're in San Francisco it would not work well to advertise in San Francisco for a performance you're giving in New York. As mentioned before, having a free ebook with useful information will entice people to go to your site.

This ad will be picked up by Google and generate some extra traffic from anyone that clicks on your link. You will have to renew the ad as it will only be active for 7 days, but you can repost every two days.

I've also had some success posting in other areas on Craigslist but the Bay Area is the best at the moment.

It's worth noting that although some areas do not get indexed as fast by Google it might still be worth it if your ad is allowed to be active longer. For example, the Orange County section of Craigslist will not be indexed as fast but they allow your ad to be active for a much longer period of time.

# Chapter 18
## ▸ MySpace and YouTube Bot Marketing

If you are worried that you won't have the time to market your music or promote your band the way you want, there are alternatives that can help reduce the amount of time you spend.

The world of bot marketing can save hours of hard work by automating the process of communicating with the rest of the network.

I should state right now that it isn't a tactic well-received by the MySpace and YouTube community. To reap success with bots, you have to know how to disguise yourself and work stealthily.

If you overstep the mark, they will delete or block your profile. You can probably imagine how devastating that would prove after months of carefully planned promotion. It is important not to spam, and to be respectful of MySpace and YouTube policy.

The reality is that many people make use of bots successfully and I want to give you a full scope of the options available to you. The benefits if used cautiously and wisely are plentiful.

You don't HAVE to use bots to be successful. But as your marketing efforts grow you might find that the time saved with these bots are well worth it. For those who want to, this chapter will help you along the way.

## SOFTWARE TO TURN HOURS INTO MINUTES

Having seen how many options there are on MySpace, it's not an understatement to say that marketing on this web site is a time-consuming business.

There are many reasons why you might not have the time to engage in a carefully developed campaign. Third party developers have caught on to this and as a result, there are a growing number of bots which specialize in automating the MySpace and YouTube experience.

They handle everything from accepting friend requests, to sending out hundreds of messages at a time. There are also bots to increase your MySpace song plays and views. There is even a bot to increase your video views on YouTube. The most appealing use comes from the software's ability to run for hours on end without you even being at your computer.

You can come home from work and find your MySpace profile with hundreds of new friends, song plays and views.

You can be successful using the strategies we covered in this book, but if you want success in a shorter amount of time, using a bot may be another choice.

A Google search of "MySpace or YouTube bot" is likely to return a large number of these particular programs. They all hover around the same price. Some bots are free, but you'll rarely find a free one which offers a full array of features.

If you're going to go with a MySpace bot, you might as well choose one which can handle messaging, comments, bulletins and friend requests. You can also get specific bots for increasing your song plays and views quickly.

One Bot called "Tune Boom Pro" will increase your views and plays on MySpace and also your video views on YouTube. You can find it at the URL below:

- http://www.tuneboompro.com

It's very simple to use and an effective bot will help you get results fast. In addition they can also provide the service for you if you don't want to do it yourself.

It should be noted that increasing your song plays on MySpace or video views on YouTube will not only be a factor in getting a higher position on the MySpace charts or being chosen as a featured video on YouTube, but more importantly as others notice that you are getting lots of plays or views, they will be curious and want to see what it is all about. It becomes a snowball effect. If you are perceived as being very popular, people will not want to miss out and many will want to be included.

There are a number of these products available and the prices are generally pretty competitive.

It's a bargain if you're looking at things from the perspective of how much exposure you're going to get for your money. I can tell you now that you'll get more than you would without it. If you are busy working full-time, running your own web site or store, and trying to find time to perform and write songs, you may want to use bots on MySpace and YouTube to automate the routine tasks.

 Alert - Your account has been blocked due to suspicious activity. If you feel it has been blocked by mistake, please Click Here

### *The result of a failed bot campaign*

If MySpace detects that you're abusing its system, you can expect to say goodbye to your messaging privileges.

The above will be displayed above your inbox and your account will be closed.

This is one of the dangers associated with using bots. MySpace and YouTube has been cracking down on them so don't abuse them.

You have the opportunity to unblock your account by clicking on the message from MySpace and usually they will unblock your account providing it has not been grossly abused or you have been spamming everyone. DO NOT SPAM! Be respectful and you will be able to use these bots effectively.

# USING THIRD PARTY BOTS

Most bot software is easy to use once you understand its functions. The idea is to automate certain aspects of MySpace and YouTube marketing, so it makes sense that they shouldn't be too complicated.

You'll normally have to register your software before its activated and ready to use.

It's also worth noting that most bots are installed on the operating system. MySpace or YouTube will be accessed within the program but the software itself is downloaded to your local computer. This means that you can only use it on one system, although there's no limit to the number of accounts that can be wired into the bot's workings.

Open up your program and you'll typically find a window pane to log into your account, and another sidebar for account options. Each piece of software is different. Some programs such as the ones increasing your song plays or YouTube video views do not need to be logged into your account.

Think of the bots as modified web browsers with additional options.

The best bots on the market will provide functions for:

- Adding friends
- Sending messages
- Posting bulletins
- Accepting friend requests
- Posting comments
- Increasing song plays
- Increasing views

You will be asked to provide details for your account if the software needs to log into your account. This is to automate the process of logging in.

Next, you can pick your account from the pre-set list and log-in. You'll notice how the bot now does this for you based on the info you provided earlier. You will not have to enter your details every time.

Once you're logged in, you'll receive confirmation.

Some Bots work by extracting MySpace IDs. Every user has a unique key assigned to them. The bots extract these IDs from each page and put together a list of IDs in a temporary database.

You can then program an action, such as a message. You input the subject and the body of the message, and when you start the sending process, the bot will send that message to every ID that it's extracted.

*The MySpace search criteria*

So what is the best way to extract these IDs?

Bots will automatically scan for user IDs based on search criteria you have entered or a specific user ID that you can input. It makes sense that if you're going to target a specific group of users, you should use the search feature as shown in the screenshot above. You can also search for other bands similar to your band and then request their friends to become your friends.

Choose settings that are likely to return users from your target market, then press the "Update" button.

You now have a list of up to 3000 profiles! These are all members who match the search criteria. There may be more or less than 3000, but that's the cut-off limit.

Now you can simply extract the IDs with the use of the bot software. Click "Extract" or "Get IDs" depending on what application you're running and the bot will surf through every last one of the search pages. It won't stop at the first page. The software is designed to detect multiple pages of search results and it will collect every last ID.

Stop when you feel like you've collected enough. Now check over your message details and when you're happy, press "Send."

The bot will go through and send your message to every last one of the extracted IDs. The recipients won't know that you've been sending messages via a bot, so expect a full inbox when you return.

As you can imagine, this saves a LOT of time. How long would it take to cycle through and message 400 users in one burst?

With the help of a bot, you can go out and let the software do the hard work for you. It doesn't matter what you're doing, the bot will cycle through every last profile until all of the messages have been sent. It will skip any errors and duplicates.

You can do the same thing with comments and even friend requests.

If people want to add you as a friend, you can configure the bots to automatically accept requests.

With some programs, you can go as far as to send a friend request AND a complimentary message.

Just remember, there are limits to how many you can send in one day before MySpace considers your message abusive or spam. They might also ask you to input a Captcha code after the first 50 messages or friend requests to confirm you are in fact a human and not a robot. Be careful and don't abuse this!

The bulletin system is slightly different than what you'd expect, it serves up more flexibility. By using an automated bot, you can write bulletins in advance and have the bot send them out when the time arrives.

## AVOIDING THE BLACKLIST

If marketing could only be as easy as pushing a button and letting a bot do the hard work, we'd all be using them.

Unfortunately, it isn't.

As already mentioned MySpace is pretty strict about members abusing its service with bots and third party software.

Avoiding the blacklist should be a number one priority if you're going to be using automation software.

A few things to consider:

Currently, you can only send a maximum of 400 friend requests in a day. MySpace considers it unreasonable that anybody should be THAT sociable that they need to send more. If you overstep the mark, you're likely to find yourself at the top of their suspicious list.

There is a strategy to get around it somewhat. Although you can only send 400 requests, that doesn't mean that you can't accept more that 400 requests sent to you.

If you create a duplicate account, you can use it to send messages to people with a link in the body. These are messages, NOT friend requests.

The text should act as an invite to add you. But you should code the URL so that when they click the link, they don't add the account that the message came from, they add your real MySpace account instead.

This is a brilliant way to add friends to your genuine profile without risking the prospect of landing on the blacklist.

The recipients aren't likely to know any different either. Make sure you use the same display picture, profile and name for your duplicate account.

Using this discrete technique, you can add thousands upon thousands of friends every single day. If MySpace looks in on the sudden growth, they'll only see that members have been adding you. Not the other way around. After all, you're inviting users to send a friend request—not initiating the process.

Considering the most popular bands receive thousands of adds every day, you'll escape the penalties.

But again, I must caution you that these strategies are at your own risk! They can get you banned and cause your account to be closed!

## GOOD MANNERS GET YOU EVERYWHERE

If you're going to send a huge number of messages, make sure the body of your message is friendly and warm. If you come across as a robot, you're likely to get reported in a hurry.

I would strongly recommend that you send no more than 100 messages at a time. MySpace will detect if you're sending large batches of messages, and as we saw above, they're not afraid to block your account from further activity. If you get blocked, there's little you can do.

Moderation is the key as far as avoiding the blacklist. If you set up your software to send out messages 24/7, you WILL get blocked.

Furthermore, once your account has been blocked, all of your messages will be deleted from the system. Even the messages that have already been sent; they'll be replaced with a "This profile has been deleted" alert. `MySpace keeps a tab on account activities. It should be noted that if too many people report you for spamming, you're likely to have your account closed. As I said before, it's imperative that you keep things friendly.

Even if you can't attract new fans, at least word your pitch in such a way that they'll be happy to ignore you. The last thing you need is complaints filed against you!

# HOW TO APPEAR GENUINE

One of the most important things about your marketing approach is that you sound genuine.

If you reel off catchphrases and slogans, you can expect minimal success. Remember that there's a time and a place for broad stretching advertisements. It's fine to be impersonal when you're advertising through a television commercial. People don't expect to be addressed personally.

But when you send messages in to somebody's personal inbox, they expect to be addressed on a personal level. Otherwise, it's rude.

If you're going to use software to send bulk messages, spend some time hand-crafting a message which seems relatively conversational.

Don't break into your sales-pitch right away. You should come across as friendly and interested in the recipient. You don't have to know their name, but ask them how they are. Ask them if they've had a good weekend. Do whatever it takes; just make the effort to distinguish yourself as somebody who is interested in more than their patronage.

By using this method, you can expect a lot of replies. Asking questions is a great way of avoiding the junk heap. If somebody replies with a friendly comment, take that as a sign to drop your sales pitch.

After you've set the bot software to send out your messages, give it a rest for a little while.

Cycle through your replies—you will receive them when you send messages on a large scale like this—and respond with genuine interest. If they care enough to send a message back to you, you should be able to strike up a good relationship with them. Ignore anybody who replies with abusive material. It's not worth pursuing.

## Chapter 19
▶ **Protecting Your Music On MySpace**

The social networking sites described in this book are secure web sites that you can post your music on. But that's not to say that there aren't malicious users out there who take great pride in sabotaging the hard work of others.

Sometimes your music can be compromised by fans who genuinely mean well. On other occasions, you can find yourself the target of theft. Either way, it's important to know how to protect your music.

In this chapter, we'll be looking at how you can protect your music on social networking sites. You'll see how the support system works and I'll address several copyright issues that you might need to face up to at some point in the future.

## LEGAL ISSUES WHEN SHARING SONGS

If you've had your eye on the news, you are well aware that sharing songs over the Internet is a controversial issue.

Lawsuits have been filed, companies have gone bust, and the recording industry has faced a complete overhaul.

In 2006, there was a great deal of concern amongst artists about a small passage in the MySpace terms and conditions. It read as follows:

> *"You hereby grant to MySpace.com a non-exclusive, fully-paid and royalty-free, worldwide license (with the right to sublicense through unlimited levels of sublicenses) to use, copy, modify, adapt, translate, publicly perform, publicly display, store, repro-duce, transmit, and distribute such Content on and through the Services."*

The clauses lead to a great deal of speculation over what hidden rights MySpace was trying to claim over their members' music.

MySpace has since moved to quell such concerns. They amended their terms with the following paragraph:

> *"MySpace.com does not claim any ownership rights in the text, files, images, photos, video, sounds, musical works, works of*

*authorship, or any other materials (collectively, 'Content') that you post to the MySpace Services. After posting your Content to the MySpace Services, you continue to retain all ownership rights in such Content, and you continue to have the right to use your Content in any way you choose."*

You can upload your songs without fear of giving away the rights to them.

## WHAT IF SOMEBODY STEALS MY MUSIC?

MySpace cannot be held responsible if your song finds its way on to somebody else's hard drive.

It can, however, take responsibility if a member decides to upload a song and host it against your wishes. It's not unknown for users to add songs to third party players instead of using the standard media player.

It can be hard to track such instances and the only viable way of uncovering illegal sharing is by stumbling onto the infraction or by somebody else bringing it to your attention.

Some fans are particularly obsessive about bands that they like. Try to be diplomatic in the way that you go about handling such a breach of copyright. They might not even realize that someone can download your song from a player they are using and are just being supportive.

More often than not, the problem can be solved by sending the user a polite message and asking them to remove your song.

Provide a link to where the track can be purchased legally (where applicable), and be on your way.

If the user fails to heed your warning, or you believe they are profiting from your music without your permission you're within your rights to contact the MySpace support team.

Make sure you check the status of your sent message. If it says "Sent," the user hasn't opened it yet. If it says "Read," and it has been read for a considerable time, the member hasn't taken your warning seriously.

At this point, you can file a complaint to the MySpace management and they will go to the necessary lengths to ensure that your music is removed from the offending user's profile.

I recommend taking the polite course of action first. It's not worth upsetting your own true fans any more than you need to. At the same time, don't let stray members get in the way of your marketing plans.

# FAKE TRIBUTE PAGES

You may have noticed when searching for a band on MySpace, there will be an official profile along with any number of unofficial tribute pages.

The main purpose of these accounts is to fool users into believing that they're adding the real deal and get the traffic from the affiliation. Whatever the reason, such pages can be a nuisance if you're looking to keep a cohesive brand identity on MySpace.

If you find that somebody is imitating your work, it's best to message them directly and ask for their immediate removal of your details. This will usually result in the complete deletion of the profile.

If the user doesn't respond, feel free to contact the MySpace support team. Staff members spend an unreasonable amount of time deleting duplicate profiles, so you may have to wait a few days before anything is done.

The upside to fake tribute pages is that you'll be reaching out to a much larger audience than you originally intended. If MySpace members are happily promoting your work on their own accord, this could be interpreted as free marketing. But it rarely works out like this and it can actually harm your long term business strategy.

It's also confusing for your genuine fans. They may begin to question which profiles are official, if any.

Not every duplicate artist page is out to leech from your talent. There are some genuine fans who simply don't understand the workings of the Artist Sign-Up feature. They might be trying to provide a community for discussion of your work.

If this is the case, message them kindly and explain the situation. Suggest that they show their devotion by setting up a MySpace group instead. It's possible that they're genuine followers of your work and simply need another way to express themselves.

Chapter 20

# ▸ What's Next? Music Industry Thoughts

It is important to think about where the business model will be in the years ahead, so you can prepare yourself to be ready for all the changes that are sure to happen. They will affect how you do business dramatically. While no one person can predict with absolute certainly what the changes will be, we can be certain things will be different.

That doesn't mean, however, all the lessons learned will no longer be valid. Some will remain as important as they are today, others will need a new twist on them, and others might simply not be effective anymore.

As you market your music more and more, you will develop a sense of what works and what does not. PAY ATTENTION! If you stay aware of what is going on and what is working for you, you'll never feel out of touch and you will easily adapt.

As this book goes to print, iTunes is the third largest music retailer in the U.S.A.—behind Wal-Mart and Best Buy. Unlike Wal-Mart and Best Buy, iTunes gained share despite the fact it only sells downloadable content, and it leapfrogged CD-heavy Amazon. The top 5 stands as follows:

1.  Wal-Mart (15.8%)

2.  Best Buy (13.8%)

3.  iTunes (9.8%)

4.  Amazon (6.7%)

5.  Target (6.6%)

I thought it would be fun to list some ideas that many in the industry feel could be the "New Music Business" of the future.


## ADVERTISMENT SUPPORTED MUSIC

Imagine a future where you have access to an unlimited source of music, without connecting to a computer or having to upload to your device. Music players will be on a network where you can find all music. Hit play on your iPod (or phone, or any device), and listen to the music. There will be some kind of an advertisement experience there, which the labels will get a percentage of as revenue. People are going to expect that they can get anything whenever they want to.

# SOCIAL NETWORKING CONSUMER

Social Networking will be integrated with retail. Within a text message, IM, MMS, or email a friend can say, "check out the new XXX single," you can click on it and listen and get more info. If you like it you can hit * plus a code and buy it instantly. Maybe you bought it from the artist and not even a label! If the price point is low enough, it will allow consumers to buy at the moment of impulse. Social Networking is a natural for this.

# MONTHLY PAID SURCHARGE

People will pay a monthly surcharge on their cable bill for example, and download an unlimited supply of music. Songs are being downloaded in the billions already. That is a huge market that can be tapped into not by trying to change a behavior but by creating a business around it. You already pay your cable company for services like HBO or a level of basic cable, and music will be another tier. These companies can administer the royalty payments made from pools of money collected and distributed based on stat rates or voluntary rates.

# REDEFINED MUSIC LABEL

Labels will operate more as agents or managers, earning their profits from licensing, touring, and merchandise. The record label design that exists today is an artifact of the physical sales model. As physical CD sales continue to decline, the labels will work more as venture capitalists, much like the film industry operates today, essentially as business partners. If the artists succeed, then the labels succeed. In a digital world, this is a way to align the interests of the artist and the label.

# ► Conclusion

We all have different goals, both financial and creative. You might simply want to use MySpace to earn extra income on the side, or you might desperately want to quit your day job so you can work on your music full time. Or you might be thrilled to have built a large loyal fan base, who love your music and attend your shows. You can reach your goals by using MySpace and the other social networking sites, and the strategies in this book are the tools to get you there.

You've learned how to make full use of the features that social networking sites have to offer. It's easy to be intimidated and feel overwhelmed with all the particulars of creating profile pages, uploading materials, and all the music marketing strategies in this book.

The important thing to remember is that even the most popular musicians had to start somewhere. It takes commitment, but if you follow through you will be well ahead of the many that never do. If you've come this far, you've already proven that you're committed to doing what it takes, and are willing to put the work in.

We can't pretend that having incredible music won't go a long way to determining your level of accomplishment or super stardom, if that's what you're after. It's the key ingredient to your success. But if you believe in your music and you want to touch people's hearts with your songs, it is crucial to make sure that people can find them and listen to them.

You now know how to specifically use social networking sites, article marketing, podcasts, RSS feeds and the many other strategies in this book as ways to optimize your chances of success, both with a record label and on your own.

Use these strategies and your music will be heard.

Patience is another tremendously important element of your campaign. I've highlighted how it's possible to go from a new profile with zero friends, to a large list of friends in a matter of days, even hours. But I can't stress enough that real success takes time.

It's easy to lay the foundations of an effective marketing campaign, but you have to be willing to hang in there with sustained effort over time. If you don't get the desired results in the first few days, don't let that be a red flag that you're doing something wrong. Marketing will continually build on the day before. This is particularly relevant if you're trying to attract the eye of a record label.

A&R scouts and agents can take a great deal of time to locate new artists. Currently, it seems as if things are moving away from the traditional A&R model and towards a model of picking up artists that have a proven track record on their own, whether that be sales history, radio play or a strong fan base. Even if they do find you early, it's still likely that they'll undergo a great deal of discussion internally and track you, sometimes silently, to see how you go about your business. Success HAS been found on these sites, and it will continue to be that way.

If you're an independent artist looking to go it alone, there has never been a more exciting and opportune time in the history of the music business. I'm pleased to offer you my thoughts about how to get noticed in the music industry via one of the most comprehensive books on this topic available. The Internet has already helped many young and seasoned musicians along the way to independent success and I hope that you consider the marketing techniques in this book wisely.

Reliance on record labels is no longer the only option you have. Expect to see this shift in power continue over the coming years. There could soon be a time where the music landscape is dominated by artists who control themselves creatively and commercially. This is something I'd very much like to see.

I welcome your comments and stories. There is nothing more gratifying than knowing you have helped someone in the pursuit of his or her dreams.

Email your thoughts, questions, testimonials or queries about other subjects you would like to learn about at the address below:

vip@MySpaceMusicProfitMonster.com

I wish you the best of luck with your music marketing venture, and in pursuing the opportunities that it brings. I thank you for the opportunity to share my thoughts.

To your personal and musical success!

Bonus Chapter A

# ▸ Basic HTML Codes

Use these codes to customize your text, images and overall look. Most of these codes will work on any site that allows you to use HTML such as Squidoo and MySpace. You can use, for example, the text codes when you send a bulletin on MySpace to change the text to be larger. It's also a good way to test your code as before MySpace sends the bulletin it gives you a preview. Before the preview it will just look like code.

## TEXT CODES:

- **Bold text:**

    `<b>`Your Text Here`</b>`

- **Italicize text:**

    `<i>`Your Text Here`</i>`

- **Font size:**

    `<font size=Your Font size Number Here>`Your Text Here`</font>`

- **Strike through text:**

    `<s>`Your Text Here`</s>`

- **Underline text:**

    `<u>`Your Text Here`</u>`

- **Line space break:**

    `<br>` Your text Here`</br>`

- **Standard text link:**

    `<a href=Your full destination url>`Your link text `</a>`

(This does not open in a separate window)

- **Standard text link that opens in a new window:**

```
<a href=" Your Full Destination url " tar-
get="_blank"> Your Link Subject </a>
```

- **Font color:**

  Use an Html color code chart to enter the color of your choice where it says "Prefix #."

  ```
  <font color=Your Color Number>Your Text Here</
  font>
  ```

- **Font Style:**

  ```
  <font style=Your Style Name>Your Text Here</font>
  ```

- **Start a new paragraph:**

  ```
  <p>Your Text Here</p>
  ```

- **Centered text alignment:**

  ```
  <center>Your Text Here</center>
  ```

- **Left text alignment:**

  ```
  <div align="left">Your Text Here</div>
  ```

- **Right text alignment:**

  ```
  <div align="right">Your Text Here</div>
  ```

# Image and Link HTML Codes:

- **Add a image:**

  ```
  <img src="Your Image url" height="0"
  width="0">
  ```

- **Add a image and specify a width and height in pixels:**

  ```
  <img src="url_Of_Image" height="20px"
  width="20px">
  ```

- **Add image link:**

  ```
  <a href="">Your url <img src="Your Image url"></
  a>
  ```

This allows you to have any image you want to use, active as a link, so when someone clicks on it they are taken to your web site, blog, order page etc.

- **Add a image link and set the image height and width:**

```
<a href="Your url"><img src="Your Image url "
height="0" width="0"></a>
```

- **Put a border on a image:**

Change the "Your Html Color Code " to the color you want and choose one of the "solid|dashed|ridge|dotted" border styles:

```
<img style="border-color: Your Html Color
Code ; border-style:solid|dashed|ridge|dotted
; border-width:3px;" src="Image url ">
```

- **Make a thumbnail link:**

```
<a href="Your url"><img src="Your Image url
Here" width="200"></a>
```

## BUTTONS:

- **Make a "Add Me" button with a image:**

Add your friend id# after "friendID=" where the XXXXXXXXX is below.

Insert your picture url and your back link text.

Then insert the message you'd like people to see :

```
<a href="http://www.myspace.com/in-
dex.cfm?fuseaction= invite.addfriend_
verify&friendID= XXXXXXXXX " target="_blank">
<img src="Your Picture url" alt="ADD YOUR
MESSAGE HERE" width="85" height="85" bor-
der="0"></a><br><b>ADD YOUR MESSAGE HERE</b></
p></center>
```

Bonus Chapter B

# ▸ HTML Codes For MySpace

These are MySpace specific. Simply go to edit profile and paste the code in the appropriate section. You can test your code using the bulletins as outlined in the previous chapter.

Unless otherwise stated, the codes below can be inserted into any section on the interests & personality page.

## Remove AND HIDE Sections

- **Remove URL box:**

```
<style type="text/css">table table table ta-
ble div {visibility:hidden;} div table table
table table table div input, div a, td.text
div visibility:visible;} </style>
```

- **Remove extended network box:**

```
<style type="text/css"> table tbody td table
tbody tr td.text table {visibility:hidden;}
table tbody td table tbody tr td.text table
table, table tbody td table tbody tr td.text
table table tbody td.text {visibility:vis-
ible;} </style>
```

- **Remove general information:**

```
<style type="text/css"> table td.text {vis-
ibility:hidden;} td.text td, td.text span,
td.text a {visibility:visible;} </style>
```

- **Remove details:**

Put this at the bottom of the heroes section:

```
</td></tr></table></td></tr></table></td><td
><divclass="hidethem"><table><tr><td><table>
<tr><td>
```

Put this at the beginning of your About Me form:

```
<style>.hidethem {visibility:hidden; display:
none;}</style>
```

- **Remove friends:**

```
<style type="text/css"> td.text td.text
table table table, td.text td.text table br,
td.text td.text table .orangetext15, td.text
td.text .redlink, td.text td.text span.btext
{display:none;} td.text td.text table {back-
ground-color:transparent;} td.text td.text
table td, td.text td.text table {height:0;pad
ding:0;border:0;} td.text td.text table table
td {padding:3;} td.text td.text table table
br {display:inline;} </style>
```

- **Remove comments:**

This goes in the city line of your Basic Information page.

```
<div style="position:relative; height:400px;
overflow:hidden; border:0px;"> <table><tr><td>
<table><tr><td>
```

- **Remove friends and comments:**

```
<div style="display:none"> <table><tr><td><ta
ble><tr><
```

- **Remove only the comments link:**

```
<style>td.text td.text td td a, .redlink,
td.text td.text td b a {visibility:
visible!important;}td.text td.text td a {vis-
ibility:hidden;}</style>
```

- **Hide display name:**

```
.Hide {user:name}
```

```
.nametext {display:none;}
```

- **Hide default photo:**

```
table table table table td.text a img {dis-
play:none;}
```

- **Hide blogs:**

  ```
  table td table tr td.text table {visibil-
  ity:hidden;} table td table tr td.text table
  table, table td table tr td.text table table
  td.text {visibility:visible;}
  ```

- **Hide "Who I'd like to meet":**

  paste into The "About Me" section:

  ```
  </td></tr></table><table style='display:
  none'><tr><td>
  ```

- **Hide your MySpace URL:**

  ```
  Hide {profile:url} table table table table
  table div strong{display: none;} table table
  table table td div {visibility: hidden} table
  table table table td, table table table td
  {background: transparent;}
  ```

- **Hide the music player:**

  ```
  td td embed { display:none }
  ```

- **Hide contact box:**

  ```
  .contactTable {display: none;}
  ```

- **Add a background:**

  ```
  <body background="http://www.yourdomain.com/
  image.gif">
  ```

- **Add a section:**

  ```
  </TD></TR></TABLE></TD></TR><TABLE><P><TABLE>

  <TR><TD><TABLE>

  <tr><td class="text" valign="center"
  align="left" width="300" bgcolor="6699cc"
  height="10" wrap="" style="word-wrap:break-
  word"><span class="whitetext12">Write your
  Title of the section here</span></td></
  tr><tr> valign="top"><td><table bordercol-
  or="000000" cellspacing="3" cellpadding="3"
  width="300" align="center" bgcolor="ffffff"
  border="0"><table border=1 cellspacing=1 cell
  padding=1><tr><td>Write your text or contents
  here</td></tr></TABLE>
  ```

- **Automatically resize comments:**

  Add this code to the end of your "about me" form field and the comments will automatically resize so you don't have comments with huge images.

  ```
  <style type="text/css">

  td.text td.text table table table td a img
  {width:100px;}

  td.text td.text table table table td div img
  {width:80px;}

  td.text td.text table table td img
  {width:260px; max-width:260px; width:auto;}

  td.text td.text table table td div img
  {width:80px;}

  * html td.text td.text table table td img
  {width:260px;}

  * html td.text td.text table table td a img
  {width:90px;}

  * html td.text td.text table table td div img
  {width:80px;}

  </style>
  ```

- **Find a friend ID number**

  From any profile page you can find the friend id# by looking at your browser:

  http://profile.myspace.com/index.cfm?fuseaction=user.
  viewprofile&friendid=XXXXXXXXX

The number at the end is the unique friend ID number.

# ▶ Testimonials

"Call Nicky. See if he can help us with this." How many times have I heard this over 20 years? Many, many times—from record company presidents, from A&R executives, from various heads of record label departments. With his years and years of studio expertise, A&R experience, and knowledge of so many facets of record company workings, Nicky Kalliongis is one of the music industry's true "go-to," "turn-to" executives. And now, as the head of his own label, Moda Records, Nicky has kept the hits coming with Anna Vissi and Helena. It is no wonder that so many in the music industry "call Nicky."
**—Michael Barackman, Music Consultant, former Senior Director A&R Arista Records**

"Nicky K is the best! We worked together at Arista and Nicky was absolutely instrumental in helping me with edits for Santana's groundbreaking "Supernatural." We couldn't have done it without him. He's also a great A&R guy who has made some amazing records. Go Nicky!"
**—Pete Ganbarg, President, Pure Tone Music**
**former Senior VP, A&R for Epic Records and Senior Director, A&R for Arista Records**

"Nicky has been a big part of a lot of hits for me: Crystal Waters, Cathy Dennis, Seduction, 98 Degrees, etc.—a true pioneer!"
**—Bruce Carbone, Executive VP or A&R**
**Universal Motown Records, Universal Records**

"I worked side-by-side with Nicky K and watched him apply his studio skills. Whenever we left the room, the track sounded much better than when we walked in. He has considerable knowledge about the ins-and-outs of the recording studio from the technical and creative points of view, and any music-business aspirant should benefit from hearing his tales from behind the industry scenes."
**—Mitchell Cohen, former Senior VP, A&R, Columbia Records**

"I've known Nicky Kalliongis as a go-to guy, someone who can enhance music into the best it can be, while maintaining the artist's vision. He is a seasoned professional and someone that I can always rely on."
**—Tom Mackay, Senior Vice President of A&R Universal Republic Records**

"I have known Nicky for over 15 years now even though it seems like yesterday that he took over Arista's studio. He has the same love of music, the same passion, the same drive and the same thirst for excellence today that he had when we first met. He lives and breathes music and these days that's a rare characteristic for an executive. The artists he's been involved with read like a Who's Who in Contemporary Music.

While shooting the cover for *Whitney: The Greatest Hits*, Clive Davis stopped by the session to play a demo of a song that would become yet another Top 10 hit for Whitney. Huddled in a corner listening and giving their reactions to the song were Arista's founder, the top female artist of all-time, and a beaming Nicky Kalliongis. I don't think that smile ever left his face."
**—Ken Levy, Former Senior Vice President, Arista Records**

"Nicky K is an expert in pro-tools editing. We created hit single edits for Whitney Houston, Toni Braxton, Exposé, Snap, Deborah Cox and the Ultimate Dance Series among many others. Nicky K is a true professional in every sense of the word."
**—Hosh Gureli, Vice President A&R, RCA Music Group**

"In addition to being the eyes and ears of industry icon Clive Davis, Nicky Kalliongis has worked with some of the biggest names in popular music. Whether it was artists such as Whitney Houston or Kenny G, Nicky worked at the very highest levels of the music industry. Nicky Kalliongis is the #1 go to guy in NYC...he makes stuff happen...period!"
**—Avery Lipman, Sr. Vice President, Universal Republic Records**

"Nicky is a multi-talented musician and A&R person. Having worked closely for industry legend Clive Davis and on projects from the biggest names in the business from Streisand and The Stones to Usher, Aretha, Whitney, and Pink to name a very few, Nicky has a wealth of creativity and knowledge to share with any new artist trying to break through. And, he's a real good guy."
**—Michael Schwartz, President, Michael Schwartz Creative Group Inc. former Senior Director, Creative Services Arista Records**

"For the past decade, Nicky has been the guy to go to and an excellent A&R man. Always ahead of the game, and clearly stands out as one of the most forward thinking people in this industry. He is incredibly talented, hard-working, and has a wonderful spirit."
**—Sal Guastella, Senior Director of A&R, Universal Motown Records**

"I've had the pleasure of working with Nicky Kalliongis at Arista Records. Nicky has worked with many hit recording artists, from Whitney Houston to international star Anna Vissi. With his excellent track record working with the biggest artists in the music business, Nicky adds much value to today's artists and their music."
**—Peter Visvardis, Sr. Director of A & R, Zomba Music Publishing**

"I have so many interesting stories about Nicky I don't really know where to start. The fact that he was Clive Davis' personal A&R man was pretty amazing. I mean, how cool is it that an industry legend and the last of the true record men wants you're opinion on what to sign?

This was all very behind the scenes and not for public consumption so keep that under your hat.

Nicky was a staple at Arista for so many years, it was like he was there when they opened the doors and left when Clive Davis was unceremoniously ousted…it was still about the music back then and not about big corporations running everything.

Nicky was at home doing A&R but had a pretty big recording studio right above Clive's office where artists would come to record promos, edit or just hang out in a studio. Everyone loved Nicky because he was so down to earth.

You can always tell the guy who loves his job because every minute of everyday, it's like he just started, with all the joy and wonderment of a kid in a candy store.

I remember when they were doing song edits on 1/4-inch reel to reel players where you'd have to cut the tape and past it together. Talk about a specialized skill…it's part technician, part seamstress, part chef and all focus.

Nicky could do edits that no one else could do. There were many times where he would do a test edit and send it to Sterling sound to be re-cut and mastered and he would have to go over and do the cut again…those guys couldn't duplicate what he did.

Nicky was also a published musician, wrote music for TV shows and had an artist deal with Atlantic Records (I'd pay money to see those publicity photos). He also owned his own recording studio and record label (when he had time for all of this, I'll never know). Everyone knows who he is and he's one of those guys that makes everyone smiles when his name comes up. Nicks career coincided with a time when music was a visceral, living thing that needed the human touch of a master craftsman who respected both the art and the artist. Now, all you need is a computer and an idea. Nick is like vinyl…real, fragile, warm, layered and rare.

The fact that these types of men are the first casualties of the digital era is not only a sad thing for me, but a tragic day for music.

In a time when everyone can be famous (and it seems everyone tries), true talent can fall by the way side but only for a minute. As long as music connects with people on a emotional level like no other media, men like Nicky Kalliongis will be involved, be it producing, promoting or teaching.

The libraries are full of instructional manuals on how to succeed in the record business. Nicky is a walking, talking, encyclopedia of music knowledge and experience…its about time someone was offering unique insights to those looking for truth over hype, patience over popularity and sincerity above all else."
**—David Santaniello, Senior Vice President, Strategic Marketing & Business Development, Columbia Records**

# ▶ Acknowledgements

A creative endeavor is never the product of one person. I want to acknowledge and thank the following people, in no particular order, for their inspiration, friendship and help.

Clive Davis for your incredible passion and for being a tireless and demanding tutor. Thank you for professionally and personally always being available to me.

Monte Lipman for the altruistic support and being someone I can always count on for help connecting the dots.

L.A. Reid for always being accessible to me and sharing your knowledge and thoughts so freely.

Donnie Lenner for your continual steady adeptness to triumph where others would have given up.

George Levendis for the extraordinary advice and input.

Dave Santaniello for always doing the "Right Thing" and unfailingly being there.

Todd Wagner for including me and letting me experience so many incomparable transcendent moments that have had an enormous impact on me. I'll never forget it. Without fail, I walk out of our meetings a little more capable than when I walked in. Thank you for guiding me more than you probably realize.

Mark Cuban for being genuine and authentic, unafraid to put yourself on the front line. Thank you for the massive inspiration. Your enthusiasm is incredibly infectious and appreciated.

Ken Levy for being someone that I trust. Watching you run the Creative Services department at Arista was amazing! Thank you for your insightful advisement.

Michael Barackman for being an encyclopedia of music. I can always count on you in so many different musical arenas.

Richard Sweret for delivering great music internationally. It is my great fortune that we are working together.

Hosh Gurelii for countless hours in the studio. How tremendously rewarding it is to be thousands of miles overseas and see the crowds go crazy listening to the remixes we have worked on together.

Pete Ganbarg for the remarkable time we shared in making some records.

Richard Sanders for being receptive, responsive and offering advice.

Mitch Cohen for sharing your familiarity and observations.

Bruce Carbone for your considerate and professional reinforcement.

Avery Lipman for putting in all your effort in anything I have ever needed your help with.

Robert Wolf for being allegiant, unshakable and resolute. I could not ask for a better attorney. You always come through.

Sal Guastella for being available on IM anytime!

George Andros for being principals-based and for your persistent fruitful efforts.

Michael Schwartz for your inspiring creativity and inventive ideas.

Pete Visvardis for you spirited resourcefulness.

Dean Kaltsas for being my financial adviser and always looking out for my best financial interests.

Ursa Philbin for your insightful advice and dialogue. Thanks for your unwavering energy and enthusiasm.

Telly Hatzigeorgiou for your above-board sincerity and unquestionable geniality.

Mary and Emmanuel Kalliongis - Thank you for caring as much as anyone could imagine. I could not have been more fortunate.

Julie-Ann Amos for your tireless effort in getting this book to be the best it could be.
Clive Calvin of Comnexis Inc. for allowing me to bounce my ideas off of you, even at 3 a.m.!

Nick Faselis for your beneficence and patience.

Rock Wilk for your steadfast ability to stay focused.

Gerard de Marigny for your greathearted hospitality, mildness and accommodating acquaintance.

Jacob Hoye of MTV Books for your incredible insight and never-ending enthusiasm. Thank you for believing.

Comnexis Inc. and all the staff for their desire to publish quality action-able information that music artists all over the world can use. Thank you for convincing me to be part of it. And all the artists I've been fortunate to have the opportunity to work with.
A special thank you to all the independent and up-and-coming artists, musicians, and independent labels. Without you the music world would simply not be exciting. You are the lifeblood of this business.

In addition, the following people have generously given their expertise friendship: Jim Kalliongis, Nula Chrisohoides, Angelo Chrisohoides, Tina Hoffman, Matt Hoffman, Peter Pantelides, George Pantelides, Jimmy Pan-telides, Niko Pantelides, Valia Pagaloutou, Peter Pappas, Susan Planer, Glenn Friscia, Warren McRae, Alan Plotkin, Steven Brown, Robert Gorden, Ray Caviano, Jay Messina, Nick Cucci, and Lollion Chong.

To anyone I may have forgotten, know that I am grateful to you as well. I send a heart-felt thank you out to you and promise to get you in when we reprint.

# Also available from MTV PRESS

### THE WORLD ACCORDING PRETTY TONEY
THE AUDIO AND LITERARY EVENT OF THE MILLENIUM

"...based on a character he played in a series of MTV2 shorts...a peek inside the mind of Pretty Toney...— a sort of *Chicken Soup for the Hustler's Soul*" — RollingStone.com

### MISSHAPES

"The history of nightlife here is well-told and well-mythologized..." —*Sally Singer – VOGUE*

"You'll want to cherish this definitive document of 2007 as a historical artifact. Nothing could be a purer representation of right now than this collection of 2,000 photos...it's a time-capsule record of the most fabulous and shiniest of our age." —*Style.com*

### JACKPOT

"A survey of the color photographs that Landers made between 1990 and 2007 showcases a slacker sensibility too amused and blasé to be seriously cynical. Like a grungier Martin Parr or Tony Feher with a camera, Landers makes pictures of people and products that tease Pop mercilessly. Studio still-lifes of panhandlers' cups, three-card-monte cardboard totems, and plastic bags snagged on broken branches rescue their subjects as found sculpture.... Call it photography of the absurd, but nobody does it better." — *The New Yorker*

## Available wherever books are sold.